W9-AUO-318

PEACE FIBRES

stitching a soulful world

*Peace —
One stitch
at a time
Karen*

KAREN LOHN

With contributions from Catherine Zdechlik

INTEGRAL PRESS

GRAND MARAIS, MINNESOTA

Copyright © 2011 by Karen Lohn

All rights reserved
No part of this book may be used or reproduced in any manner whatsoever without written permission,
except in the case of brief quotations embodied in articles and reviews.

Book and cover design by
Maryl Skinner and Denny FitzPatrick, M Graphic Design, Grand Marais, MN

Photo credits appear on pages 170-176.

Published by Integral Press
P.O. Box 1181
Grand Marais, MN 55604
www.peacefibres.com

Printed and bound in Canada by Friesens
First Edition

ISBN 978-0-615-45611-9

DEDICATION

To that Thai woman on her porch whose name I know not,
and in celebration of the global community of fibre artists.
With every fibre of my being, peace to you.

WITH GRATITUDE

A tiny filament of vibrating energy, a string that caresses another, joins with the next, becomes. Like my grandmother's crocheted doilies, just one thread entwines with itself in loops and circles, continuously becoming more. One thread, this book became more through the generous and creative contributions of many, only some of whom I can name here. Those who remain nameless are, nonetheless, recipients of my heartfelt gratitude.

This symbol of gratitude, above, was created by Stacey Robyn, and led to the Go Gratitude Experiment, a project exploring the spiritual impact of gratitude.

Bob, Martiga, Darci, Andrew, Abbie, Riley, Jake

Thank you first to my base, the context out of which I live, Bob. He has been my primary support, my greatest cheerleader, my willing helpmate through the many years in which this book was becoming. And I thank my children and grandchildren for providing the life lessons woven throughout the chapters, as well as the encouragement and love that is the ground bed of all creative endeavors.

Louise, Helga, Marie, Donna, Merra, Maryl, Mary

I thank also my mothers, the one who birthed me and the others who counseled and nurtured me through life, most notably dear Donna who mothered me through a third of my life. Gratitude also to my grandmothers, Helga and Marie, whose legacies of fibre creations continue to entwine the generations as I share them with my grandchildren.

Ruth, Marjorie, Arlene, Elizabeth, Mary, Margy, Andrea, Iris, Erika, Sophie, Jan, Kay, Madge, Marie, Judie

Sisters, dear sisters…. Biological sisters, sisters-in-law, soul sisters across the globe who shared fibre stories and fibre creations and whose lives are entwined with my own through their compassionate, and passionate, giving. They are my inspiration. Great gratitude to each.

Norris, James, David Michael, Clair, Edward, Bud, Peter, Uwe, Doug, Denny

Father, brother, mentor, friend, counselor, protector. Men who blend the masculine with the feminine. My appreciation for your guidance, guardianship, and willingness to show gentleness and caring.

Linda, Jan, Karen, Kay, Virginia, Nancy, Paulette

My first readers. Each took a chapter in its early stages, critiqued it, did the projects, and gave important and helpful feedback. Special thanks to Linda who hosted the group and who took reworked sections home for careful revision. I laugh when I think how rough it was then and how tenderly you helped me rip out and reweave. I laugh when I think of how many times over the ensuing years each of you has asked, "How is your book coming?" Thank you.

Carol, Peggy, Marcy, Peg, and others

Quilters who allowed me to visit their retreat in the very early stages of my research. I appreciate your openness to sharing your stories and your stunning work.

Linda, Nina, Ann, Mary, Kay, Korey, Maxine, Karen, Tara, and many others

Members of the Northwoods Fiber Guild who opened their doors and hearts to me, inviting me to share this book's theme and encouraging me to join with them even though I only dabble. Thank you.

Bonnie Gay, Barb, Mary Ellen, Judy, Suzanne, Carolyn, Joanne

First participants in my Peace Fibres retreat who enthusiastically twisted yarns, poked needles, wrapped themselves in fibres, laughed, cried, stitched, and danced. The shawl, hats, and blanket they created warm and comfort an elder, a cancer survivor, and a sick baby. Gratitude for so zestfully engaging in the process.

Gloria, Ann, Jennifer, Joan,
Cheryl, Gail, Deb, Bonnie, Donna, Barb, Sue, and others

The Fabric Series participants. Thank you for coming out all those cold evenings to connect the threads, and your lives, with one another and with me.

Manuela, Alyssa, Juanita,
Angelina, Carlos, Patti, Jan, Peter, Viktor, Gabby

Part of my Mayan experience in Mexico. Batik on the beach. Back-strap weaving. Hand-embroidered *huipiles*. Water, waves, wax, work, wonder. My gratitude for all that you taught me on so many levels. Peace.

Tomas, Dianne, Masumi, Uwe, Iris, Sandra, Jill, Patty

Thank you for opening your homes and your studios to share your wondrous fibre collections, creations. Your stories are an integral thread in the fabric of this book. I am grateful.

Erika, Brenna, Miriam, Jo, Leslie, Carin, Barb,
Marge, Kathleen, Angela, Karen, Marge, Ellie, and others

Artists who participated in an exhibit, "The Gifts and Metaphors of Fear: Pulling the Wool Over Our Eyes," in Superior, Wisconsin. Your interpretations inspired me. Your willingness to share with vulnerability was moving. Thank you.

Dr. Daina Taimina

For so generously sharing her model of hyperbolic space, uniting the world of science with art. Much appreciation.

Mary Carroll Moore

My first editor/coach who gently coaxed my voice, corrected my errors, and guided me onto the page. Gratitude.

Bud McClure and Erika Mock

For reading and critiquing the early manuscript, then writing endorsements. Your support and encouragement over time has been invaluable. Thank you, thank you.

Jan Sivertson, Beth Kennedy, Lee Stewart, Joan Drury,
Cameron Norman, Linda Zenk, Jody Thone, and others

Business women who supported this book, offering advice and opportunity to spread the word. My appreciation.

Bea Sorenson and Sarah Zdechlik

Proofreaders extraordinaire, wise women, and friends. Thank you for lending your "eagle eyes" to ascertain quality.

Friesens

For the fine service, guidance, and expertise in making the actual book even more beautiful than imagined. Gratitude.

Artists who shared images

Requesting permission to use images of artwork provided an amazing witness to the generosity and goodness of artists and photographers across the globe. Over 100 of them on six continents granted permission. Their enthusiastic encouragement, willingness to take extra steps to provide the images, offering more was profound. For those whose work we were not able to include and for those we did, much, much appreciation.

Organizers of fibre cooperatives across the globe

Gratitude for the work you are doing to empower through the economic valuing of fibre creations.

The woman in Thailand whose name I do not know,
the batik circle in Java, and
the silk workers in China

Thank you. You opened my heart and my eyes.

SPECIAL THANKS

Catherine (Katie) Zdechlik

Longtime friend whose eye for beauty, precision with words, and wise counsel provided the warp through which the chapters are woven. Her additions to the text add color and texture to the fabric of the book. Her willingness to research, review, critique, and help me rewrite provided sustenance to continue. Katie's "scrunch ball" gift captures the thesis of *Peace Fibres*. My loving appreciation.

Maryl Skinner, Denny FitzPatrick

Willingness to wrap herself in a cocoon of blankets, don a flowing fuchsia "Sophia" dress, arriving barefoot with champagne, Maryl's immersion in the process of this book gave it life. Her creative genius is evident on every page. Denny's amazing technical skills and his patient willingness to respond to the creative whims of Maryl and myself made manifest the vision.

Together they embody the integration of the masculine with the feminine in wondrous ways. I am profoundly grateful to both for their months of intense design work, research, and editing of this book, and for the years of new friendship ahead. Thank you.

CONTENTS

INTRODUCTION

The Big Bang, batik by Karen Lohn

Joining, connecting, uniting. Creating harmony. Making beauty. Beginning with a simple basic fibre — a string, a thread, a yarn, a cord — relationship undulates as one thread entwines with the next and the next. Cooperating with the artist and with one another, sometimes challenging, each contributes to the whole until a fabric emerges. A garment. A canvas. Fibre work is both metaphor and manifestation of peaceful interdependence.

Theoretical physicists suggest that everything in the universe may be composed of infinitesimal vibrating filaments of energy — strings. Superstring theory! Could little threads offer a great unifying model for developing a more soulful world?

The human being is the only creature not clothed sufficiently for the elements — we borrow fibres from the animal and plant kingdoms in a relationship of interdependence. Human hands weave science with art, creating yarns and fabrics that build connection between individuals, cultures, and nations. Knit or crocheted blankets and prayer shawls comfort the injured, the sick, and the dying; the unique fibre art of tribe or nation connects generations; creative design, color and texture of fabrics contribute to the beauty of our bodies and our homes; mittens, scarves, and jackets protect us from the elements.

Can the very act of working with fibres serve as an avenue toward peace within an individual? Many believe so. Engaging the body and mind to knit, weave, crochet, or stitch prohibits demands from the outside world; the focus is on the present, the now. Entering a creative mode, rhythmic needles singing, the stillness of focused attention is meditative. People who feel centered are more likely to emanate peace.

The sense of accomplishment in creating a garment or work of art increases an individual's self-worth, empowering that person to contribute his or her unique gifts to the world.

Therapists are harnessing this health-inducing activity into their practices, offering knitting and spinning groups. School teachers are introducing fibre work to young learners to enhance intelligence, strengthen self-esteem, and develop social skills.

Indeed, fibre work serves the entire range of Maslow's hierarchy of human needs, from basic subsistence to self-actualization, and even beyond, to spiritual connection. It unifies. Those who have the luxury of fibre work to meet the higher needs are invited to reach out to those who weave and sew for the very basic need to survive.

Across the globe, women's economic cooperatives are emerging and giving handmade, homespun fibre creations in developing countries value in the marketplace. Though there may be a danger in simply becoming part of the existing economic system, the cooperatives are exactly that. They work to empower women.

Fair-trade organizations strive toward equity for the farmers and ranchers who raise the animals and plants that provide the fibres, as well as for those who do the spinning, weaving, and sewing. Until we meet our basic needs—food on our tables, a roof over our heads, clothing on our bodies—we cannot hope to reach our fullest potential individually or collectively.

Animal rights activists work to protect the creatures from whom the wool, the silk, and the hide are gathered. Sustainable practices are taught and encouraged for growing the flax, the cotton, the hemp. The emphasis is on a relationship of mutual respect for Earth and for all the creatures that inhabit the planet with us. The United Nations designated 2009 The International Year of Natural Fibres. Its goal is to support and encourage global awareness of the importance of natural fibres.

I am not suggesting that we burn our manufactured

"**Ultimately, we have just one moral duty: to reclaim large areas of peace in ourselves, more and more peace, and the more peace there is in us, the more peace there will also be in our troubled world.**"
—**Etty Hillesum (died in Auschwitz at age 29)**
 An Interrupted Life

Women's cooperatives, like these in Morocco, and in Peru (at top), empower women and provide economic support for their families.

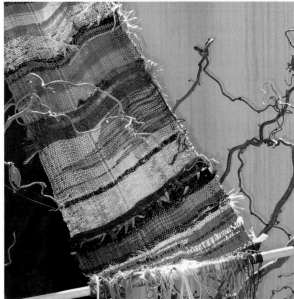

Andi of British Columbia demonstrates *Saori* weaving, a style dedicated to free expression and self-development. It has been used to make peace banners.

textiles, or return to homespun as Gandhi did; synthetic fibres and mass production serve many important needs. Advanced technology has made possible medical feats few of us would reject; still, people turn to complementary modes to call back the soul of healing. I am suggesting that handmade fibre work pro-

vides a complement to manufactured textiles, offering an integration of the archetypal feminine with the masculine.

We are in global crisis. At least 20 wars exist across the globe at any time; with nuclear weapons spreading, the madness intensifies. Violence disrupts families, communities, nations. Greed ravages the Earth and its people. The chasm between the wealthy and the poor widens in geometric ratio, much as the elimination of planetary species occurs. Individuals attempt to fill emptiness with addictions of all sorts. Obesity has become a national epidemic. With all the advances in an unbalanced patriarchal world, we are yet a mess.

Where is the integration of the right-brain feminine with the left-brain masculine? Compassion, connection, community, cooperation, creativity, and contribution are essential to the achievement of internal and external peace. These are relational qualities and are all expressed through fibre work. Dr. Jill Bolte Taylor, neuroanatomist who writes about her personal experience through stroke, states, "…our right mind perceives each of us as equal members of the human family. It identifies our similarities and recognizes our relationship with this marvelous planet."

Unfortunately, as cultures evolved from egalitarian to patriarchal dominance through the industrial age, the division of labor along gender lines relegated handwork with fibres to the realm of "women's work." It was discounted in value, as were the associated feminine personality characteristics. With mass production of textiles and garments, the "soul" of fibre work diminished.

Seems we long for that lost "soul." September 11 spawned a major revival of the fibre arts of our grandmothers, evidenced by thriving textile centers, guilds specific to each art, and a plethora of journals. *Peace Fibres* invites your participation in reclaiming our individual and collective souls. Use the chapters as catalyst for reflection, discussion, and action.

Each chapter is fronted with a symbolic fibre photo, and a prayer for peace from one of 12 traditions. These prayers were offered at the United Nations International Year of Peace in 1986. Copying is encouraged.

THE WORLDWIDE WEB

Fibre creations evolve as human needs evolve. Clothing, canvas, and nets protect us from the elements and help provide food. Sensory awareness is enhanced through appreciation of the textures, dyes, and fragrances of fibres and their sources.

Our sense of competence is enhanced when we create something useful and beautiful. Connection to others takes place as we share fibre creations or our love of a fibre technique or process. Awareness of unique cultural identities and contributions through fibre work instills appreciation for diversity. Awe at the intersection of science and spirit with art demonstrates the interconnectedness of all.

Cast on one tiny string, twist and loop, connect another…and another…and another. Like this vibrant Paraguayan *ñandutí*, fibre work entwines all in ever-expanding compassionate connection to self, others, the larger world, and beyond.

Ñandutí, this Paraguayan lace, illustrates the radiating web of fibre connection. Women of Paraguay capture the fractal patterns of nature by gracefully stitching layers connected to layers in a durable web of beauty and strength.

A Radiating Web of Fibres

Self • Fibre Creations
Meditative awareness/creativity/competence
Intrapsychic

Nature • Fibre Sources
Animals and plants/human-made
Interdependent

History • Art of Grandmothers
Fibre techniques/identity
Intergenerational

Others • Fibre Contributions
Family and friends/intimate connection
Interpersonal

Global Fibre • Commonalities
Diverse cultures/awareness, appreciation
Intercultural

Cosmos • Fibre Art
Unity/science, art, spirit
Inspirational

Chapter 1

WEBS OF CONNECTION

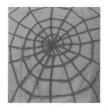

Shinto Prayer for Peace

Although the people living across the ocean surrounding us,
I believe, are all our brothers and sisters,
why are there constant troubles in the world?
Why do winds and waves rise in the ocean surrounding us?
I only earnestly wish that the wind will soon puff away all the clouds
which are hanging over the tops of the mountains.

Spider web on Isle Royale, Michigan

WEBS OF CONNECTION

Weaving done by this Thai woman supports her family.

The young man helped us down from the unsteady saddle of the elephant. I was nervous riding atop that powerful animal. Though logic told me he had done this zillions of times, I was more comfortable managing the rough dirt paths on foot. Protruding tree roots treaded the steps sloping upward into the wooded village. They seemed familiar, like the trails through the Boundary Waters of my northern Minnesota home, and I recognized the fragrance of decaying vegetation becoming soil.

Little else was familiar. With my sister Beth, I was adventuring through the Far East, at this moment visiting indigenous villages of hill tribes in northern Thailand. Beth travels the globe, garnering multicultural awareness. She invited me to accompany her on this sampling of life in Southeast Asia.

We had motored up the Mekong River among lush, fragrant hills and low green mountains, guided confidently by Canadian Maria who had spent a decade working in these communities. Two young men were waiting at the dilapidated dock when she cut the motor and eased our small craft toward the waiting elephants.

With little fanfare, they led us to a platform and onto the huge elephant's back. Beth was seated behind me. We made jokes about last wishes. I felt my heart pounding. One young man prodded the elephant with his baton and our host plodded forward.

Maria walked with the young men, chatting amiably as Beth and I touched jungle tree tops and hung on for a short rhythmic ride to the Karen village near the top of the slope. There was another platform waiting for our dismount.

Small bright-eyed children and thin dogs scurried around us, the children asking for a coin — "one baht." They had become accustomed to the curious presence of tourists in their otherwise isolated dwelling place in the mountains. Their voices, and an occasional yap from a dog, were the only sounds in this quiet nonmotorized village. Adults greeted us with nods or smiles. Some seemed not to notice our presence at all. Maria explained that the use of opium was a continuing social issue in the area and the subsequent loss of productivity from many males contributed to the poverty of the tribe.

We walked into the "streets" of the village, dirt paths lined by rough-hewn slat homes. Bamboo trunks were held together with hemp cords to create walls and structure for the roof thatching. Most had porches protruding in the front. We watched children playing, men talking, and women weaving on the rough porch floors.

One blackened-tooth woman lifted her head to smile at us and beckoned us over. We stood at the edge of her porch as she shifted the simple backstrap loom on which she was working, and moved the basket of threads and yarns to show us her creation. It was a long thin stretch of striped fabric, alternating rough ivory threads with narrow bands of rosy red and sky blue. The skirt she wore over her dark leggings was nearly identical but for the darker colors in deep red with one band of purple. A woven bandana crowned her head.

The woman beamed as we attended to her work; she seemed pleased by our appreciation. She gestured to the covering on her floor, another woven stretch of material, green and beige. Then she pointed to the lean-to off to the side of her house where hung an entire fleece, as yet uncarded and unspun. A spinning wheel stood waiting.

Maria explained that this woman was the family breadwinner. Her handmade items would be sold at the local market to tourists such as us. When I asked if I could buy something directly from her, Maria discouraged me, saying that the central market had been organized to better serve the tribe economically.

Beth and I, through gestures, thanked the woman for welcoming us and for sharing her work. How I wished I spoke her language. How I wished I had learned her name. We then continued walking through the village,

"All things are connected like the blood that unites us. We did not weave the web of life, we are merely a strand in it. Whatever we do to the web, we do to ourselves."
—Chief Seattle

observing other weavers at work along our way.

That afternoon we arrived at the open-air market. In the large thatched cabana we discovered not only table runners, sashes, bags, and rugs woven in a similar striped pattern, but jackets with bands of the same flat weaving decorating the cuffs and the zipper fronts. We learned from Maria that each of the hill tribes has a distinct identifying weave; the Karens are known for bands of ivory and rosy red with accents in primary colors. The Akha tribe adds colorful pompoms.

I selected jackets for my daughters, added another for myself, each with the distinctive band of Karen weaving. I also purchased a long rough-textured beige table runner, with stripes in rosy red. It adorns my table today as I write, reminding me of my connection to that remote area of the world, to that woman on the porch who proudly and competently created it, contributing not only to the well-being of her family, but my ongoing pleasure.

Beth and I traveled on to other villages and tribes, witnessing the importance of fibre work as creative outlet, economic necessity, and contribution to the well-being of others. We purchased symbolic items from each area. As we trekked on to Bangkok, Hong Kong, and Indonesia, we were surprised by the vital role that fibre creations served. Fibres spun into threads entwined with other threads, becoming fabric, evolving into art, clothing, and coverings spread across the globe.

When we arrived in Jakarta, a meeting of Asian Pacific Economic Cooperation (APEC) was taking place, with heads of state from 18 nations, including U.S. President Bill Clinton. Extra security was everywhere—this helped us feel a bit safer since women traveling alone are regarded warily in this Muslim country. We wanted to see a performance of the Rama-

Intergenerational Javanese women counsel and support one another as they use their *tjanting* tools.

yana, hear Gamelan music, and visit tea plantations. I was also interested in seeing batik art.

The Gamelan music was soul-soothing and the Ramayana was resplendent with its colorful costumes and animated story. We did tour a tea plantation. However, not until our driver took us into a small, somewhat dilapidated old warehouse was I transformed.

The scent of candles — beeswax melted for the batik process — wafted through the open doorway. Soft Gamelan music served as background for the scene we were witnessing. Inside the unpainted, rough timber building, 12 Javanese women, ages 13 to about 70, sat on low stools with wooden racks of large muslin draped over them, hot pots of wax smoking beside them, deftly directing their *tjanting* tools, turning cloth into glorious designs and patterns. Each wore a pink smock to protect her clothing from the hot wax and the dyes, the pink incongruous with the bare-bones lack of softness in this work setting.

There was an obvious matriarch — long gray hair

pulled into a bun, wire-rimmed glasses covering her wise eyes. A young woman with child sat beside her, absorbing the wisdom that the elder woman exuded, much as the cloth absorbed the dye. Two other artists sat slightly removed, talking in low tones with occasional laughter accenting their intimacy.

While the group worked, talked, laughed, and obviously counseled one another, I suddenly knew that this was what I had come to witness: multigenerational women in community, expressing their competence creatively through fibre art, earning a living, and serving one another in a relationship of support, humor, and wise counsel.

This is the connection that I had been sensing in all the other visits, in the purchases I had made along the way. That day I realized: Feminine wisdom is sustained through the generations by working with fibres. An intricate, complex, and amazing web is woven among women — across generations and cultures.

The next morning Beth picked up a copy of *The Jakarta Post: The Journal of Indonesia Today.* On the front page was a full-width photo of the 18 heads of state, Bill Clinton in the center. Each was wearing a beautiful, unique shirt in the subtle colors of Indonesian batik. It was symbolic that the leaders of many nations, all males, turned to the expressions of beauty and creativity done by the women. Patiently, it seems that women have been warming the world in spite of the devaluing of their art, in spite of patriarchal exploitation, in spite of abuses. We could only ponder how the world will be different when a balance of women wear the shirts and men participate in creating them.

• • •

Home now, in the chill North Woods, I host a retreat of friends and sisters, a loose-knit group of intergenerational women seeking spiritual depth, playful connection, intellectual stimulation, and avenues for contribution. At this particular gathering, Anna, Marie, and Arlene have come to work on small quilts to contribute to the Linus Project, providing reassurance to children in hospitals.

Ruth, Sarah, Madge, and Sophie are crocheting colorful squares of yarn for afghans, which will be sent to Afghanistan to lessen the hardship of people in that war-torn country. Baskets of bright yarns and bits of fabric accent the floor and couch on which they work. Amelia sits on the floor in the center. Grieving a marriage turned sour, she concentrates on a piece of needle felting. She is not yet ready to talk to us about the sting of her husband's request for a divorce after so many years, but she does seem comforted by our presence around her.

Katie has a knitting project. Jan and I serve as gofers and providers of refreshing drink, nourishing food. The fire crackles, fragrance of fresh mulled cider and hot cinnamon rolls drifts among us.

On the wall behind the quilters hangs my Hmong tapestry depicting the animals and plants that nourish another land; on the couch are my multicolored pillows from the market in Hong Kong. My batik tablecloth covers our food and beverage counter.

As fingers stitch and twist yarns, we talk and laugh and counsel one another. I tell them about my trip to the Far East. I tell them about the batik in Java and point out features of the work on the tablecloth and napkins we are using. I fetch the silk that I brought from Hong Kong and the jackets from the market in northern Thailand. And, I focus on how powerfully I was touched by the woman on her porch weaving with

"Women's work is always toward wholeness."
—May Sarton

a backstrap loom to feed her family. We talk about learning names when we travel to make personal our communication. They quickly see the many connections woven among the strands of the various cultures Beth and I visited.

Jan tells me about a batik workshop on the Yucatan Peninsula that she will be teaching with a Mexican batik artist. I have wanted to learn the art of batik ever since visiting Java, and a vacation on a beach in Mexico sounds appealing, especially since I am already planning to travel to Chiapas, a nearby state, as part of a church delegation standing in solidarity with the struggling indigenous communities there. Amazingly, the two events are consecutive, so Jan and I decide to do both together. Again, the role of fibre will be a focus for both experiences. I want to learn about Mayan textile art, particularly weaving, that continues to be a major economic resource for people of the villages. I am excited.

Suddenly, Katie, our naturalist and observer, hushes us. She points to the window overhang just outside our cabin. A very large spider is patiently weaving a web. It is glistening from the fresh morning rain, radi-

Heads of state, including President Bill Clinton, pose in traditional batik shirts, woven by Indonesian women.

Cocoons of silkworms transform not only the life of a tiny larva, but the politics, economics, and social fabric of a nation.

The golden orb spider emits a thin thread into the wind, allowing it to catch onto a branch or other object. It then repeats this until a 'Y' is formed—three bases for the strong, enduring web, much like our bases of mind, body, and spirit. The web is so strong it can even capture small birds; it endures often for several years.

"From common threads, a world of strength and beauty we can weave."
—Unknown

ant in the rays of sunlight just appearing. We watch her patiently, diligently, purposefully creating this web of delicate fibres which will provide food for her body and offspring. The web's sunlit beauty astounds us.

I notice cocoons of other small creatures hanging in the window box and I am reminded of the silk worm whose cocoons transformed not only the tiny larva inside but the politics, economics, and even marriage practices of a large nation.

In this moment, the interconnectedness of all things is clear: the cocoon, an individual life protected by fibres, allowing solitude in order to undergo transformation within, much like our grieving Amelia; the spider connecting strands to provide sustenance for her family. Fibres are amazingly strong and resilient; unraveled, they become threads of silk, prized by humankind like the small quilts offered to young ones who are ill. Woven together, the threads become glistening fabrics, receptive to color and offering beauty as well as warmth.

How like fibre artists across the globe, throughout the ages! Like the woman on her porch in Thailand, quietly, patiently, transforming selves into strong, competent providers, protectors, and artists. United through the fibres with which they work, providing not only beauty, warmth, and intimate connection, but also transforming economies and politics and cultures. Often discounted, ignored, even destroyed, this resilient, nurturing wisdom persists in a glistening web of interdependence, of relationship.

Substance. Fibres. Fibres connecting, connecting through fibres. Peace fibres.

Silence as each woman returns to her fibre creation. Needles poke and twist the threads, the yarns. Pattern develops as the sun drenches our weekend.

The work has taken on increased significance. There is an unspoken awareness that these projects are a contribution to peace, from the healing of an individual's grief to the collective message of compassion for the suffering of a nation.

THREADS FOR THOUGHT

•In Greek and Roman myths, fibre work was designated a feminine activity while metallurgy was considered masculine.

•Hestia was the Greek goddess (Vesta in Roman mythology) of the hearth, center of the home and even of the community, tending the fire and all the care of the household. This included provision of clothing for all members; thus spinning, weaving, and sewing were all considered feminine activities.

•Sigmund Freud reportedly stated that the only contribution women made to civilization was that of "plaiting and weaving." If so, is it not the warp on which much of humankind is woven?

•In hunter-gatherer societies, the power structure of males and females was relatively egalitarian, and in horticultural societies, matriarchies occurred. As we moved toward agrarian (plow farming) economies, however, with land ownership and the marketplace for commerce, women's unpaid work in the home declined in value. The industrial age separated the genders even further, especially in middle- and upper-income families, as males regularly left the home for work.

•As mass production swept the textile industry, hand-produced fibre creations declined while sweatshops exploited cheap labor to turn out bolts of fabric and garments to be exported across the globe. While nearly everyone now had access to an array of products, the "soul" of the work had been removed from the creator.

•Advances in communication and transportation have reduced distances between and among cultures. Access to information, products, and peoples is available globally—but only to those with wealth and power. These advances lean heavily toward masculine characteristics, including autonomous achievement, competition, and logic. They often neglect the importance of building relationship in concert with technology.

•Peace involves relationship to self, to others, and to the larger cosmos. The feminine qualities expressed in fibre work—care, connection, cooperation, compassion, creativity, contribution—are all about relationship.

•How will our lives be different when these become equally valued and lived in partnership with the masculine characteristics?

•How will we be more fully functioning individuals when we develop both dimensions of ourselves?

For many decades, mathematicians struggled to develop a model of the geometric phenomenon called "hyperbolic space," which has opposite curvature to a sphere. It was a female mathematician, Dr. Daina Taimina, who accomplished this model by crocheting it! The intricate fibre art, above, is at the Smithsonian Institution.

CONNECTING ACTIVITIES

Fabric sculpture by "Jo" of New Zealand

Threads of transformation will connect you to the fibre of your own soul. From there you'll radiate from your center point toward others in your life and the larger world.

• • •

Preparation, patience, and persistence are required for fibre projects. Peace also. Peaceful connections begin within, then radiate outward in ever-expanding ripples.

"Connecting Activities" in each chapter are designed toward this goal. I believe that great peacefulness is elusive in part because we spend so little time in this focused connection; the demands of our too-busy lives consume our minds, dictate our bodies, and kidnap our spirits.

Set aside a time each day for this kind of connection, like you spend time each day brushing your teeth. I prefer dawn. It sets the intention for the entire day.

"You cannot have peace just by sitting down and negotiating or making plans. You have to learn to breathe in and out to calm yourself, and you have to be able to help the other person to do like you."
—Thich Nhat Hanh

Inward connection—
C-A-L-M-Sh-h

C · Center, courage, connect. Spin the fibres. Reconnect to body.

A · Awe, awareness, action. Create a vision. Reconnect to mind.

L · Love, laughter, light, life. Cast on the yarns. Reconnect to spirit.

M · Movement, music, meditation. Join the threads. Experience union.

Sh-h · Solitude, silence, smile. Savor process. Be present.

Interpersonal connection—
Giving and receiving

Presence
Listening, validating, encouraging, accepting

Nurturing touch
Directly or indirectly nurturing

Teaching
Sharing wisdoms, resources, ideas, knowledge, spaces

Presents
Handmade, thoughtful creations from the Self

Contribution
Monetary, time, talent, leadership, presence

Interpersonal connection—
Global community

Learning · cultures, values, contributions, traditions

Experiencing · trying new things, exploring novel ideas

Competence · developing the full potential of all

Risk taking · speaking up, stepping outside of comfort

Creativity · tapping deeper, trusting inspiration, sharing

Leaving a legacy · leaving the world a better place

ACTIVITY · WEBS

Practice these breathing and focusing exercises daily this month.

- Go to your closets, cedar chests, walls, attics, and basements. Identify fibre connections that have contributed to your life's tapestry. Collect a few and spread them around you as you sit for a few moments in reverie. Is there something from another generation? Another culture? A close friend or relative? Handmade by you? If you are participating in a group, introduce yourself through these items.

- Select a soft, comfort fabric or blanket such as polar fleece; wrap yourself in it like it is your own private cocoon. While snuggled in this warm blanket of solitude, pay attention to your breathing—follow the air through your nostrils, flowing through the esophagus, and into the air sacs of your lungs. Release the carbon dioxide and smile.

- Take another deep belly breath and imagine life-enhancing oxygen flowing easily to each eager cell in your body. Exhale and smile.

- Continue following your breath and visiting your body while wrapped in your snuggly cocoon. Smile with each deep exhalation.

- Imagine all of your cells, tissues, and organs connected in a peaceful web.

- Then, shed the cocoon, stand, stretching as tall and as wide as you possibly can. Plant your feet wide and firmly and stretch your arms with fingertips reaching toward the heavens. Take up as much space as you can. Breathe and smile as you feel your strength and your expansion.

- Imagine fibres of silk exuding from your fingertips and toes, connecting you to each of the fibre items you visited earlier—connecting you to other generations, to other people currently in your life, to other cultures, to your spirituality. See the web expanding and entwining with the webs of others. Imagine the glistening dew on this web of interdependence with the first rays of dawn illuminating its beauty.

- Breathe and smile. Move as your body directs you, perhaps humming "The Peace Song."

Nootka woman in cedar bark blanket, c.1916

Choose one activity per week this month to connect outward.

- Select one item from your collection and investigate the stories contained within its threads. Who created it? From what culture? For what purpose? What is the source of the fibre from which it has been made—animal? plant? chemical? How did it come to you? What does it mean to you?

- Search the Internet for information regarding spiders, webs and cocoons. Share it with a child in your life as you examine any webs or cocoons in your basement, your window areas, or your yard.

- Which fibre best describes your temperament and personality?

PROJECT • WEBS

This "web" borrows from Native American dream catchers and also the World Wide Web, both of which connect in every dimension. See the short piece following this project.

Prepare

Look up the words to "The Peace Song" composed by Sy Miller and Jill Jackson in 1955, for the United Nations first World Day of Peace following World War II. Or, access a recording of this song offered by many artists, including Vince Gill, the Boston Pops, or Dino Kartsonakis. It begins with the words, "Let there be peace on Earth and let it begin with me." Hum, sing, or play it as you work on this project!

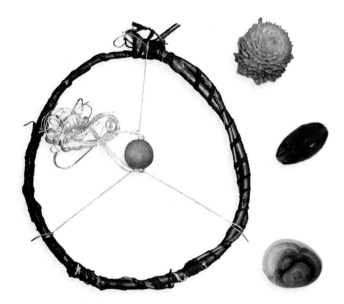

You will need

- One flexible, fibrous limb such as willow or dogwood, about two feet long. Be sure to thank the plant from which you take it. This is your connection to nature.
- An array of yarns, threads, cords, beads, buttons, small keepsakes and discarded items from nature, plus some large needles and scissors.

The process

- Firmly bring the narrow end of the limb around to meet and overlap with the wide end, forming a circle.
- Twist the narrow end around the wide end fixing securely with a "twister." (A pan lid and a few clamps can firm up the hoop shape.)
- Cut a two-yard length of heavy yarn or cord. Tie one end at the top of your hoop, which has now become a circle representative of the Earth.

- Wrap the yarn in a spiral around the hoop until you meet the place at which you began.
- Tie off the end of yarn by forming a slipknot from which it can hang.
- Select a large bead or other object that has a substantial hole through the middle. Let this object represent you.
- Cut four lengths of string, one yard each. Using a large tapestry needle, thread all four strings through the central hole in this object.
- Tie a knot that joins the eight strands around the bead. Place "you" in the center of the Earth's hoop.
- Fix in place by tying three strands to the outer hoop at approximately one-third intervals, forming a "Y" like the golden orb spider.
- Select objects now from those you gathered that symbolize connections you felt as you sat with your fibre items during meditation. Think interpersonally, intergenerationally, interculturally.
- String these onto the remaining loose strands, securing with knots or by wrapping the items.
- Now create the web by twisting over, under, and around the three secured strands and one another. As a strand is in place, tie it to the hoop.
- When all objects are attached and secured, trim loose ends.
- Hang where you can sit in contemplation of your web of connection—to self, to others, to the Earth, and to the cosmos.

OF WEBS AND WORDS

When I say the word "web," what is your first image? Employing Freud's free association technique, Americans today would likely start with the idea of the matrix of information-sharing made possible through computer technology, the World Wide Web (the Web). Perhaps this will quickly branch to thoughts of the quote from Chief Seattle at the beginning of this chapter, which may lead to thoughts of arachnids, which may trigger the adage, "Oh, what a tangled web we weave when first we practice to deceive." Webs are exactly this: intricately woven threads of connection—to people, ideas, information, objects, words.

In the late 1980s, physicist Tim Berners-Lee invented the computer code that has become the Web, with the intention of developing a tool for collaborative communication. He was knighted for donating his program in service of global understanding. What an amazing web of communication he has offered! And, with it, new words—many of them using an analogy to fibres.

Search the Web for "fibers." Zillions of options appear, including fiber optics, various sources of bran and other food choices especially essential to older adults; even links to strength of character. A web of words connecting us to every dimension.

Using Berners-Lee's web to find "Native American dream catchers," the rich lore behind these creations is at my fingertips. There are a variety of presentations, and enjoyable websites including sound. The dream catcher has a long history with variations in the lore, but the overarching theme is for the web to catch bad dreams while allowing good dreams to slip through. A dream catcher is often hung over the cradle of a child.

Try searching the Web for other fibre-related words or phrases. Notice the many fields of endeavor to which you will connect: the fabric of the universe, mending a relationship, spinning tales, God as weaver, surgical stitches and needles. How many other words related to fibres can you think of? Metaphor, analogy, simile, six degrees of separation. Webs. All one.

Chapter 2

FIBRES, OUR SUBSTANCE

Hindu Prayer for Peace

Oh, God, lead us from the unreal to the Real.

Oh, God, lead us from darkness to light.

Oh, God, lead us from death to immortality.

Shanti, Shanti, Shanti to all.

Oh, Lord God Almighty, may there be peace in celestial regions.

May there be peace on Earth.

May the waters be appeasing.

May herbs be wholesome, and may trees and plants bring peace to all.

May all beneficent beings bring peace to us.

May the Vedic Law propagate peace all through the world.

May all things be a source of peace to us.

And, may thy peace itself, bestow peace to all,

and may that peace come to me also.

Fresh fleece at my friend Sophie's farm

FIBRES, OUR SUBSTANCE

Fibre: from Latin "fibra," filament

1. thin thread

2. cloth or material made up of fibres

3. essential character

4. strength of character

Igor watched us coming up the long driveway to his farm. We had never met him, so my grand-daughter, Abbie, and I were eager to see what he'd think of us. Reluctantly, he wandered over to greet us at the gate. Abbie got to touch his long, gray beard, just before it was cut. We had arrived just in time to see the shearing of this old Icelandic ram.

Igor shared the farm with my friend Sophie. He would have preferred to gather more straw and manure in his coat, but Seth, his masterful shearer, ruled. Igor bawled, but bounced up joyfully once the coat was off and he could feel the cool autumn breeze and warm rays of sun.

Abbie and I walked over to touch the freshly shorn fleece. I taught her the old nursery rhyme, "Baa, Baa, Black Sheep" as we moved among the white, cream, gray, tan, and black bundles. Singing as we touched the oily, still-dirty fleeces, Abbie cried, "Igor stinks, Gamma!"

Certainly there was the musky smell of connection to the earth and its basic substance, a contrast to the disinfected homes in which we live. We ran our fingers through the fibres until they came out fairly drenched in the rich lanolin that renders wool its wonderful water-repellent quality.

"Soft," was Abbie's only word as her little eyelids began to drift closed.

As soon as I sat down on a hand-hewn bench covered with soft woven blankets, Sophie brought a plump clean fleece over and gently covered my now-slumbering granddaughter. She returned with a mug of savory lentil soup and a slice of freshly baked dill bread for me to enjoy while Abbie napped, warmed by the sun, the fleece, her grandmother, and the radiance of these soulful people.

Igor watches over the other sheep.

Other sheep and goats roamed the fragrant green pasture basking in the cooling of wraps-off, gathering in little groups to discuss in their own language the experience of shearing. Perhaps they were wondering what would now become of their shorn locks—much like the goat in the children's book, *The Goat in the Rug,* by Charles L. Blood and Martin Link. They seemed to be satisfied that their particular fibres held great potential once the cleansers, carders, and spinners had had their way with them.

The wall of the old farmhouse boasted the entire spectrum of yarns on sale for weavers and knitters who had only to select the colors and textures that best fit the vision of their as-yet-uncreated garments or art

Bins at Sophie's farm house overflowed with wool.

Fibre is **"a basic element that connects us organically and symbolically with the natural world. This connection is an essential one of body, mind, spirit, science, and art. We are all raw material immersed in the mystery of life."**
—Erika Mock, fibre artist

works, then to perform the magic of transformation.

Cradling a slumbering Abbie and sipping the fragrant soup, I spoke with Sophie as she worked at skirting Igor's fleece, which was now spread out on a wire frame in the leaf-strewn yard. She skillfully picked off debris and dirt. Spotting the best areas of the fleece to be captured for her spinning, Sophie exuded enthusiasm for her beloved craft and for teaching others the therapeutic aspect of working close to substance, of participating in the entire process from the rearing of the lambs, to the wearing of a self-created, handmade garment.

She marveled at the interdependence of man and the natural world to clothe humans as warmly and beautifully as creatures in nature. It seemed as though she had a wisdom from which our culture of alienation could benefit. I was happy to be introducing Abbie to an awareness that our clothing and blankets aren't somehow magically created "at the store," but require human hands and substances provided by nature.

Sophie expounded on her awe for the ingenious ancients who turned to the plant and animal kingdoms for fibres, and how they extracted, processed, and transformed these basic substances into yarns and threads and cords for myriad uses.

I told Sophie the story of my friend Masumi whose great-great-grandmother raised her own silkworms, extracted the long precious threads, wove and dyed them, and finally stitched beautiful kimonos.

Sophie explained the varying qualities offered by fibres from alpacas, goats, and rabbits. Her tone shifted to anger when she talked about the cruelties to animals that often occur in the name of profit and mass production. We talked excitedly about the Snow Leopard Enterprise that helps people living in poverty increase their standard of living, and at the same time protect their local ecosystems. The trust partners with five countries in central Asia where the endangered snow leopard lives. After careful study, the partners work with the communities to develop programs that honor both human and animal needs, with an aim toward self-sufficiency.

Perhaps the enthusiasm of our conversation or the bleating of the lambs in the distance stirred Abbie's slumber; she woke with a look of puzzlement at first, then seemed to remember where she had fallen asleep.

Smelling the table with homemade soups, breads, and cookies, she slid off my lap in that direction, soon returning with a cookie for the ride home.

Bamboo, hemp, soy, linen flax, sisal, jute, and cotton are just a few of more than 100 plant species used to produce textiles.

Mongolian herders put layers of unspun wool into their boots for warmth, shedding water, and comfort. They were surprised, arriving home after a long day's walking, that they had created a new fabric—felt—through this unintended process.

• • •

Linen as a fabric is durable and flexible; it does, however, wrinkle readily. Its fibres are strengthened by use, including rough washing on rocks by ancients or agitating in a modern machine.

• • •

Fibres are extremely sensuous, especially tactilely. Awakening to our senses is essential to becoming more soulful.

Before leaving, Abbie and I selected a small bundle of unspun wool in rainbow colors, along with some soft, clean white batting from the racks of yarns and baskets of woolen fibres to try making our own felt, a technique demonstrated by a friend. The process of turning unspun fibres into fabric through moisture and agitation seemed so simple that even Abbie could accomplish this alchemy.

Satiated and satisfied, we said goodbye to Sophie and Igor.

That night, as my son tucked Abbie into her blankie, she sighed, "We petted the 'yams,' Dadah!"

After she drifted off, I pulled out the wool I bought and set up some felt-making practice while I reviewed the day with Andy and Arlene, my sister, just retired from a career of teaching children. We talked of fibre sources—silkworms, cotton plants, flax—and of the fascinating histories of each and of how removed from these basic substances we now are.

Arlene suddenly linked the word "substance" to an old movie, *A Woman of Substance*, and immediately we both exclaimed, "Aunt Ann!" Instead of warm and cozy like the roving we had just experienced, Arlene compared Aunt Ann to silk…expensive, cold, but with beauty and sheen and astonishing strength.

Andy could only remember Ann when she was very sick, so asked for more. I recalled the tiny delicate sweater that Ann had knit for me when I was younger than Abbie. It was made of soft aqua angora, not silk.

Aunt Ann was the slim, beautiful sister of six. She had no children of her own and was twice-divorced with plenty of money at her disposal, evidenced by her wardrobe of elegant clothing and the air of aristocracy with which she moved.

Conflict moved with her. I am not sure whether some of Ann's temperamental outbursts were the result of the Parkinson's disease that eventually robbed her of motor control and, finally, her life; perhaps her sisters were jealous of her wealth and elegance, but I do know that I witnessed fights among the sisters when Aunt Ann was around.

So, I ponder, why would she knit this adorable sweater for me, her last niece in a large family with

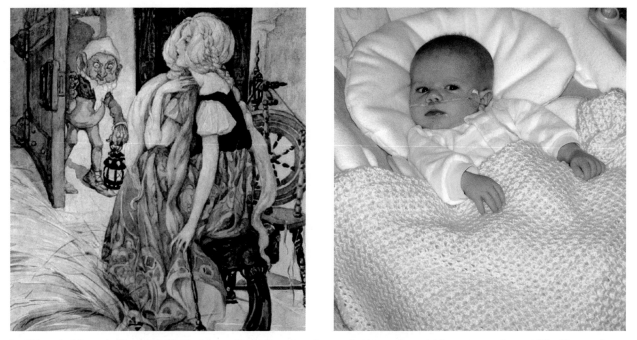

In Grimm's fairy tale *Rumpelstiltskin*, the miller's daughter is required to spin gold from straw. In real life, fibre artists transform simple substances into amazing works. Above right, Riley is warmed by Arlene's crocheted blanket.

a gaggle of nieces, including four sisters of my own, ahead of me?

I recall no affectionate connection with Ann; I cleaned her house when I was a teenager and visited her in the nursing home when she was dying. Yet, I do feel a bond with Aunt Ann because of the sweater.

I was the eighth kid in a family of nine; poverty was familiar and I lived in hand-me-downs from four older sisters and myriad cousins. I can imagine—vividly—how wonderful I felt to wear a brand-new, custom-designed sweater with tiny pearl buttons and a pocket right over my heart, though I was a toddler. Proud. Pretty.

Arlene suggested that Aunt Ann felt proud of her craft, pretty as she validated her competence even though her hands quivered increasingly as the Parkinson's disease progressed.

She borrowed the sweater to enter it in the county fair. Blue ribbon! Surely that boosted Ann's self-esteem, gave her a sense of accomplishment, and, perhaps, hope. I can almost feel the satisfaction that little sweater brought.

Perhaps, because she was childless, Ann actually had a tender spot for me in her heart. Certainly her substance, her strength of character, veiled behind the aristocratic veneer, was demonstrated through her determination to continue creating and contributing as long as she could through the ravages of her nasty disease.

"I think babies invite creative fibre work," suggested Andy, reminding us of "Baba," the old Czech immigrant who hand stitched a small quilt for Andy when he was born. That quilt became his beloved "blankie."

Andy tiptoed into Abbie's room to retrieve a yellow crib blanket with animals decorating the central squares that our longtime friend, Kay, crocheted. I can see that he retains a bond with Baba and with Kay through these creations. It is exciting to think of the bonds our brand-new grandson, Riley, will have with the aunts and friends who crocheted blankets and hats for his arrival, Arlene among them.

Andy pulled it all together as he stood up, stretched, looked at the lateness of the hour, and said, "A woman of substance could perhaps spin straw into gold, but right now I'd like to snuggle under Igor's soft fleece or even a plain cotton blanket. Good night."

Arlene and I stayed up to experiment with creating felt from the wool Abbie and I brought from Igor.

Cotton is king in the world of plant fibres. This worker is part of a cooperative project in India that markets fair-trade, organically grown cotton.

THREADS FOR THOUGHT

•The nature-versus-nurture debate has continued for centuries. The debate addresses the question of how much of who and how we are is determined by our DNA (our gene code) and how much is formed through our interactions with the environment, both human and physical.

•John Locke of the early Empiricists argued for the "tabula rasa" condition; we are born with a "blank slate" on which life writes its story through our experiences.

•James Hillman, in a popular book of the 1990s, *The Soul's Code*, proposes that everything about us is contained in that DNA code and it would behoove us to accept people as they are rather than trying to change them or, worse, blame parents for their behavior.

•Evolutionary psychologists claim that everything we do is done with an unconscious purpose of perpetuating our genes into the next generation.

•Behavioral psychologists, however, say that we are as we are because of imitation and reinforcement from others, while psychoanalytic theory proposes unconscious conflict developed in very early childhood.

•Most psychologists today accept an interactional perspective, stating that we are born with a certain temperament, most of our physical

Scarf with DNA pattern

characteristics, our talents and strengths, and probably our propensities to specific disorders and liabilities. The rest is up to us and how we handle the events of our lives.

•Ecopsychology is an emerging field that emphasizes the relationship between the health of the Earth and all its creatures and the health of our individual psyches.

•How will our lives be different when we, as individuals and collectively, accept and celebrate the diversity of sentient beings?

•How will our lives be different when our physical characteristics are experienced as simply the container for our being, a container needing healthy care and appreciation?

•How will our lives be different when we recognize that the substance of which all creatures are formed has more commonality (±93%) than difference?

•How will our lives be different when we recognize the interdependence of all the fibres of the cosmos such that we live in concert with the abundant Earth, its amazing creatures, and the peoples of the globe?

CONNECTING ACTIVITIES

"**The strategy of peace should involve practice with our body and mind.**"
—Thich Nhat Hanh

These activities can help you connect with the fibre of your own substance—body, mind, and spirit—as well as the substance of your connection to Earth, the animal and plant worlds, and other people.

Connect inward—

- Find a firm place on which to plant your feet (outside, preferably) about shoulder-width apart. Straighten your spine, raise your arms gently and slowly over your head until they meet.

- Inhale deeply, imagining air coming up from the soles of your feet through all the fibres of your circulatory system, filling your belly first and gradually your chest. Exhale just as slowly, bringing your arms back down beside your body.

- Pause. Notice every fibre in your being. Slowly name the organs and tissues in your body as you visit them with your mind's eye. Inhale again. Pause. Smile. Exhale.

- Repeat five times. Express gratitude to each part of your body for its fine work in keeping your parts connected and functioning.

Connect outward—

Return to the items you selected in chapter one, your web of connection. This time, tune into your tactile sense as you revisit each item. What is the texture and how does your skin respond to each? How about your other senses—is there a scent, a sheen, a crackle?

Which fibre characteristics best describe your temperament?

- Are you rough and sturdy, like burlap?
- Smooth, cool, shiny, like silk?
- Do you wrinkle easily, like linen?
- Are you able to repel that which you do not want to absorb, like wool?
- Do you feel misunderstood and unappreciated, like hemp?
- Are you flexible and versatile, like cotton?
- Do you take on the characteristics of others, as do synthetic fibres?
- Are you strengthened by challenges, like linen?
- Able to breathe, as cotton?
- Do you have easy receptivity, as silk?
- Are you warm, as wool?
- Are you strong as steel, like silk and many synthetics?
- Do you go with the flow as silk?
- Are you rigid, with little give, as hemp?
- Are you a blend, claiming the characteristics of many fibres?

Interactive—

- With a child, pull apart a milkweed pod, a cotton boll, or some other plant with obvious fibres. Examine them and imagine the process of preparing them for use. Encourage the child to feel and imagine with you.

- Visit a sheep or llama farm. Interview the farmers about shearing, the fleece, the joys and challenges of their work. Ask to handle a bit of the fleece if it is available. Feel the luxuriant lanolin on your hands. Hold it close and smell its earthy fragrance.

- The fibres of certain animals are prized for specific qualities. Cashmere, alpaca, mohair, Pygora. Can you discover the source of each of these fibres?

Expand—
Learn and act beyond the personal.

- Look up fibre topics on the web or in an encyclopedia. Learn all you can about these fascinating subjects, and share what you have learned.

- Explore the website for the United Nations International Year of Natural Fibres, 2009; learn about the global need for an appreciation of natural fibres and their importance environmentally as well as economically.

- Read information regarding socioeconomic or environmental concerns in the practices surrounding the production of fibres. Animal activists are concerned about the boiling of cocoons, killing the larvae, and about injury and infection that can occur when animals are sheared. Which ones awaken a fibre in your soul?

- Contact an organization that works for fair-trade practices in cotton production such as Oxfam, lobbying for cotton producers in Africa. Learn all you can about the objectives of these organizations.

- Explore the real history of cotton production in the United States. What parallels are there in the practice of "sweatshops" in the garment industry today?

Spotting (but not disturbing) a bird nest is another activity in which children can learn about fibres in nature. These eggs were laid in a cozy nest of moss, plant fibres, hair, and feathers.

Top left, Abbie shows Jake a fibrous milkweed pod. At left, Riley is about to send cattail fibres flying!

PROJECTS • FIBRES

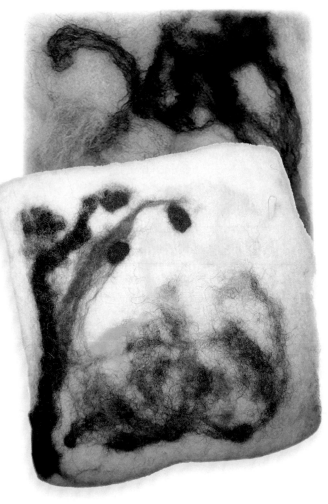

A new friend, Patty, taught Sophie and me this felting process while sharing her experiences as a nurse in South American and Mexican villages. She showed us bags, shawls, and huipiles created by the women of those villages. In addition, she told us wonderful stories of her own fibre creations, especially felting.

My fondest story is the one in which she was inspired to take a large felting project to a platform in her backyard, slip off her shoes after wetting it down, then dance on it to provide the agitation!

You will need

- A pint-sized, sealable plastic bag, an array of unspun woolen fibres in many colors, a small squeeze bottle, thimble of dish detergent, water, and patience.

- A cup of tea, glass of wine, plus a friend or group with whom to converse during this process to enhance its enjoyment.

The process

- Select enough light or white woolen fibres to lay out a square the same size as the plastic bag. Place a second layer of these same fibres over the first, with the direction of the fibres running across the first (perpendicular to each other).

- Now select a few colorful fibres and place them on top of the base, creating a design or a picture with the colors.

- When pleased with the layout, but bearing in mind that the finished product will be something a bit different—isn't it always?—carefully place the entire creation inside the plastic bag. Make sure the base fibres lay flat and completely fill the bag. Adjust the overlay fibres as needed.

- Pour the thimble of detergent into an empty squeeze bottle, then fill it with lukewarm water. Squirt this mixture into the bag with the fibres until all are saturated. Seal the bag completely.

- Now, massage, knead, pound, roll, and agitate the entire package repeatedly. This is where the wine, friends, and patience come in…or, you might dance on it like Patty!

- Occasionally, lay the bag of fibres out flat to check its progress. As you work the fibres with the moisture, you are transforming them into cloth—felt! When the entire piece is about one-half inch smaller than the bag itself and the fibres are definitely joined, transformation has occurred!

- Gently remove the cloth you have created, rinse it until the soap is out, and allow it to dry.

- This creation can become a colorful pocket on a vest or jacket, an adornment for a bag or a soft container for glasses, or it can be framed and hung.

- Enjoy your capacity for transformation and your piece of art!

SPINNING EXOTIC FIBRES

Camel-hair spinners, on a wheel in Kyrgyzstan, and with drop spindles in Mongolia, now have worldwide markets.

Sophie holds up a loosely crocheted shawl she has just finished as a gift for her daughter's bridal shower. It is formed from multiple half-circles in a variety of earth tones and textures, from flat with sheen, to fuzzy soft. Seems a curious bridal gift until Sophie explains that she has gathered, cleansed, spun, and dyed all of the yarns from animals in her daughter's life! I laugh when she points to her angora rabbit, Sugar. There's some wool from the sheep of a cousin "down under," living on an Australian farm. I am not too surprised to hear there is alpaca from the neighbor's farm, but I am astonished when Sophie says, "And this is our dog, Sassy!" Never had I considered gathering the hairs from my "grand-dogs" for transformation into garments! Yet, the ancients turned to whatever sources were available to create their threads, many of them now quite exotic.

Indigenous cultures used the strong (extremely strong!) yet generously elastic silk threads of spiders, particularly the golden orb spider, for functional purposes such as fish nets, ropes, and snares. Because it is far more difficult to cultivate, spider silk is not used for regular textiles, but is being developed with modern technology into a fabric for uses requiring extreme strength and flexibility.

Angora and cashmere were the "in" fibres for sweaters when I was young. I doubt any of us knew that those fibres were spun from goats and rabbits. I was surprised to learn about the Pygora goat's special character. Its qualities combine those of cashmere and mohair. Nomad Yarns enlists Mongolian spinners to turn Bactrian camel hairs into luxuriant yarns.

Alpacas and llamas were introduced to the U.S. from their native South America in the 1980s, becoming popular pets for families with young children. Alpacas are smaller and gentler than their llama cousins, their wool softer and denser. The warm coats of both have been worn in the Andes for centuries.

Okay, so animals of all sorts have provided fibre resources to ingenious spinners, but it doesn't stop there. Ever realized that weavers use many surprising plant sources as well—banana husks, pineapple leaves, pine needles? Most of these are labor-intensive, so anything made from these exotic fibres is unique and expensive.

I am surprised when I see a community ed class offered by a new fibre friend, Kay. Her class description reads, "Learn to spin llama, yak, dog, and angora rabbit fibres." I just giggle when I think of my three grand-dogs whose hairs clog the household vacuums and cover the black slacks I seem to constantly wear when I visit. Wouldn't it be fun to capture some of this and use it in a garment? I sign up for the class and raid my daughter's vacuum bag.

Chapter 3

SPINNING POWER
AND INNOCENCE

Native American Prayer for Peace

O, Great Spirit of our Ancestors, I raise my pipe to you.
To your messengers, the four winds, and to Mother Earth,
who provides for your children.
Give us the wisdom to teach our children to love, to respect, and
to be kind to each other, so that they may grow with peace in mind.
Let us learn to share all the good things
that you provide for us on this Earth.

Children of the World by Regal Fabrics, and Chi Chi Bear *by Chi Chi Amor*

SPINNING POWER

My eldest sister, Ruth, is visiting for a few days while I am taking care of Abbie during her parents' vacation. I show Ruth my new furniture creation, a "keeper kabinet," to store treasures of childhood, including photo albums, videos, first teeth, drawings, favorite toys and clothing, and anything else that is a memento of that child's life.

From my own "keeper kabinet" I extract fibre creations—items of innocence—done by my three children when they were young. Tenderly touching each, I show them to Ruth.

There is a plaid, brown flannel book cover made for me by my eldest—a lover of books almost from birth—who covered each of her Laura Ingalls Wilder books after reading them twice through. Next, a multicolored, small rug hooking with "MOM" lettered in the center by my second daughter. Her grandmother taught her rug hooking when she was about six, after which she made name pieces for each family member. And, a burlap bag with denim pockets, blanket stitched on each side, adorned with a pink heart and a large shiny button, created by my son, with help from his older sisters. He carried his toys in that bag when he went off to the sitter after I returned to work while he was still a toddler. Fibres of innocence so long ago.

Abbie interrupts my reverie.

It is cold this November morning. Abbie begs to play outside as the drying leaves swirl in the wind on the still acorn-strewn yard, so I bundle her in a warm jacket with cap and hood and put mittens on her little hands.

Around her throat and over her nose, I wrap a short, hand-knit, red cotton muffler. Little does three-year-old Abbie know that the scarf warming her face warmed me in remembrance of my mother. Nor does Abbie realize that the short red muffler protected her aunties in cold November winds a generation ago. A simple single scarf entwines generations. Handmade fibre garments have a knack for that.

Our mother, Louise, died seven weeks after exploratory surgery revealed advanced pancreatic cancer. I was 27. I was just beginning to grasp the enormity of motherhood, with two daughters younger than Abbie. I needed my mother and I wanted those girls to know their grandmother.

When she died, I was bereft. I was the daughter closest in physical proximity to my father's now-quiet house, so I was the one who opened my mother's cedar chest to distribute her protected treasures. My eyes blinked when I lifted the lid that spring morning. There among the long-preserved treasures of her lifetime, were hand-knit and crocheted slippers, scarves, mittens, and tiny knit tree ornaments—red stockings with white angora trim, in which a dollar could be inserted. Enough handmade items to gift each of Lou's 21 grandchildren the next Christmas!

She had labels on them already; on the red scarf was one reading "Martiga Louise," my eldest daughter, her namesake. I cried as I unfolded the simple scarf. I clutched it close, burying my drizzling nose in it. It seemed that I could smell her presence, feel her touch, see her working on this scarf as she sat on the couch listening to Lawrence Welk, perhaps dreaming of the easier life she would have chosen.

A simple, short red scarf. My mother.

AND INNOCENCE

Ruth reminds me of another intergenerational scarf. I was older than Abbie, perhaps five, when the other scarf had entwined the generations. Life in our two-bedroom house with 11 inhabitants was difficult. Dad was a loving guy when he was sober, but he often drank away the Friday paycheck, so poverty visited us along with the violent episodes that scarred our childhood.

Mom shriveled in despair and depression, yet always tried to make life easier and worthwhile for her brood of nine. I was number eight. Somehow, Mom continued to try to provide more than just food and shelter for me and all of my siblings. She remade coats from her own elder sisters, redesigned formals for my sisters' dances, and learned to knit and crochet so she could keep her kids in warm hats, mittens, and scarves during the cold Minnesota winters.

Mom kept us warm in handmade clothing.

The park across the street provided our recreation, with tennis courts, ball fields, playground equipment for summer, and a skating rink in the winter. The warming house became a haven where we could meet our friends, receive guidance from caring adults, and shine at athletic activities, especially skating. The big potbellied wood-burning stove offered respite from the cold. We often hung our damp mittens and scarves around and on it while we warmed our fingers and toes.

On the day of the scarf, I was scurrying around trying to find all my gear so I could skate with my brother at the rink. It was windy and Mom had cautioned me to "dress warm." I found everything except a muffler for my face. Mom said I could not leave the house without one. I sniffled and when Mom saw my tears, she joined my search, but was unsuccessful; the older kids had already gone off and must have taken all available scarves.

Mom opened her old red cedar chest. I can smell the sharp aromatic cedar and moth balls even as I think of it. She rummaged through a few things, pulling up an aqua and white, delicately crocheted, almost lace-like, long muffler. As she wound it around my neck and wrapped some over my nose and mouth, barely allowing room for my now-dry eyes to observe the moisture in her own, my mother said, "Ma made this for me. It's the last thing I have of hers, so take good care of it."

Off I bounced to the skating rink. Like today, it was cold that November day. Mike and I skated joyously, warm in our bundlings, for quite awhile. Finally, we succumbed to the biting chill and went to the warming house.

I unwrapped the now-wet aqua muffler, chipped off the frost, and stretched it out to dry along the edge of the big black stove. I added my mittens, then sat down to unlace my skates. In my stocking feet, I hobbled to the restroom, which was an involved process with snow pants, slacks, and underpants to undo.

When finally I was all restored, I went out to the main room, where there was a distinct smell of something singed.

I was too young to make an immediate connection. Soon someone yelled and grabbed a now brown-fringed, somewhat melted, and half-burned aqua muffler off the stove.

My heart raced. My mother's scarf—the last thing she had from her mother—she would kill me, or, worse, she would be grief stricken. I felt ashamed and sick. Skating any more that day had lost all appeal.

I put my hat and mittens and boots back on, slung my skates over my shoulder, and picked up the dead muffler. Slowly I trudged back to that too-small house of so many traumas already, gathering the courage to face another.

Mom was in the basement, shoveling black boulders of coal into the belching furnace, so I waited. When she appeared through the cellar door, she must have sensed

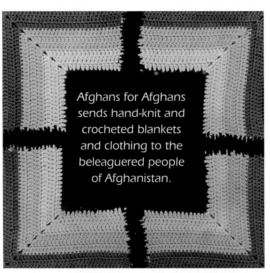

Afghans for Afghans sends hand-knit and crocheted blankets and clothing to the beleaguered people of Afghanistan.

the calamity. Perhaps she smelled the singed wool. Whatever, Mom seemed to know that I had already suffered. She picked me up, a rare occurrence, hugged me tight, and said, "Ma would have wanted you to be warm—and pretty. I'm glad you wore her scarf. Do you want some cocoa?"

Mother love. Warm scarves.

I think Abbie may want some cocoa. Ruth puts the kettle on.

She has been quiet as I talked, but now her powerful role as eldest sister, protector of her eight younger siblings and all other underdogs, wells forth. Ruth sends "throws" and bags and scarves she crochets to her sisters across the country from her California home.

First a public health nurse and then an epidemiologist who did research on AIDS, Ruth continues to do volunteer teaching for the American Cancer Society; she recently lost her daughter to breast cancer.

Ruth is the organizer of our group's Afghans for Afghanistan project, always working to contribute something for the well-being of innocent people who are caught in difficult circumstances.

Gandhi-like in her passion, not so passive in her power, Ruth's words now reflect her simmering anger

for acts of omission as well as commission in responding to the marginalized. In the next 10 minutes, her voice rising in decibels as she ignites that anger, she states the following sources for it:

- Women remain oppressed in societies across the globe.
- Even in the U.S., women in 2000 made only 77 cents for each dollar earned by men; this continued into 2011 in nearly every field.
- Sweatshop labor produces 80 percent of the clothing for U.S. consumption.
- Every 15 seconds a woman is abused in the United States.
- Substance abuse does not cause, but often contributes to, these acts of violence.
- "Honor killings" continue in a number of nations, where family members kill a woman who has brought shame on the family for being molested or raped!
- Contraceptives remain unavailable to women in many parts of the world where patriarchal dominance and religious beliefs insist on multiple children as a sacred duty.
- War adds grief and fear and destruction and loss to these already-oppressed people.

Ruth's voice softens. She then talks of the courage and sacrifice and ingenuity of women who have turned their fibre skills into sources of income as well as ordinary acts of clothing and warming the family.

Beth and I witnessed this in Thailand where we bought the jackets and table runners from the women's cooperative. The poverty of the tribes was addressed by organizing cottage industries. Women would spin and weave in their homes, and sell in the marketplace. They recognized the value tourists placed on their unique fibre creations and "spun straw into gold" by selling them to those tourists.

In rural villages of Mexico and South America, in Africa, in Turkey, in Afghanistan and India, similar cooperatives are operating. Yet, a living wage for

This "Love Blanket" was initiated by Adienne Henck and Karie Cross, as part of their work with the Advocacy Project.

handwork is hardly attainable. Manufactured textiles are more efficient.

The textile and garment industries have been among the worst in exploiting workers in developing countries. The corporate monster has no heart. It simply consumes what is in its path on the way to profit. This is an arena in which the feminine qualities of care, compassion, and cooperation are essential. The lack of value placed on "handmade" contributes to this economic dilemma.

Grassroots groups are forming across the globe, spinning gold from straw. There are long nights of spinning, and rooms of straw to be spun.

Ruth hands me a ball of yarn and a crochet hook. She insists on teaching me to crochet an afghan square for the project. It's not my thing, but I try. I am surprised by the pleasure of a single square accomplished.

"She is like a child yet is not a child. She is our mother, our daughter, our sister, our lover. She needs us now, and we need her."
—Marianne Williamson

• • •

The Advocacy Project aims at social change for marginalized communities across the globe by partnering with the community. One campaign, the Love Blanket Project in Nepal, helps create child-friendly villages in which children are free from becoming slave labor. The Love Blanket, created by Advocacy fellows and the children of the villages, symbolizes the protection a village offers its children. To learn more, visit their website.

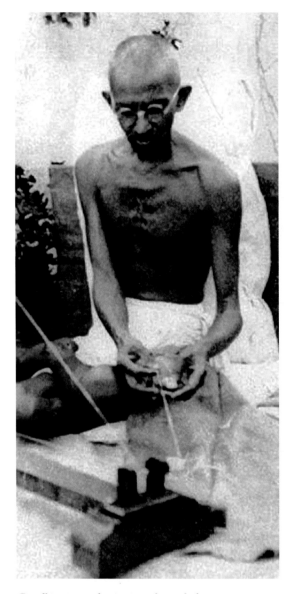

Gandhi, pictured spinning above, led a protest against British textile imports during India's struggle for independence. Gandhi himself would spin at least two hours daily and encouraged all other citizens of India to do the same. He spoke of the peacefulness he experienced when spinning. The hand-spun fibres were then woven into fabric by hand. This cloth, Khadi, *is still produced in India for traditional and contemporary clothing.*

Dating back at least 10,000 years, hand spinning is noted in myths, music, and visual arts. At right, *The Spinner,* painted by William Bouguereau in 1873. On facing page, a pastel of Gandhi by contemporary artist Sandy Frazier of New York.

THREADS FOR THOUGHT

•We come into this world with all the stuff of our DNA plus our "thrownness" into specific family, sociocultural, and physical environments.

•The family of which we are a part, the place on the globe in which we live, the events taking place around the globe, the climate surrounding us, and all the events of our lives are strands woven into the fabric of our being.

•As we develop, events occur that frighten, wound, or otherwise affect our freedom to develop fully and freely. We form our personality as a "mask" that helps us get our needs met and protects the fragile inner self.

•Whether the talents and gifts we have are encouraged or discounted depends in large part on these environmental factors outside of our control.

•Gloria Steinem states that it is never too late to have a happy childhood. This invites each of us to revisit those aspects of life that have inhibited our fullness, transforming them into strengths instead of liabilities.

•Recognizing that our personalities, our defenses, were developed creatively to serve us through our development allows us to be self-accepting.

•Understanding that these patterns may now restrict our fullest potential challenges us to unravel old threads and create new. Becoming strong, claiming our power as individuals, impacts all the threads that have formed us— our families, our culture, others across the globe, and the Earth itself.

•How will our lives be different when we claim our innocence and our power instead of hiding our small selves in shame or fear?

•How will our lives be different when aging is experienced as ripening, with the fullness of life to be shared?

•How will our lives be different when we recognize that poverty and ecological disasters and violence are not chosen by those inflicted, but require compassionate, cooperative response from each of us?

•How will our lives be different when all of us in the "have" category actively share our resources with those in the "have not" category?

Shirts made from Khadi cloth

CONNECTING ACTIVITIES

Labyrinths, such as this one at Te Moata Retreat in Tairua, New Zealand, provide structure for walking meditation.

These activities are designed to help you feel your powerful self and to cradle your innocence into strength.

"I suggest that each peace conference should begin with walking meditation...."
—Thich Nhat Hanh

"Power is the birthright of every human being."
—Rollo May

Connecting inward—
Everyday practice empowers self.

▪ Spread a soft fleece, plush throw, cushy rug, or a large towel in the center of a space where you can stretch out and move. Lie down comfortably on it.

▪ Stretch out on your back, legs spread slightly, arms at your side. Feel all the places that the Earth below supports your body. Breathe in a deep belly breath, then sigh as you release it and relax into the support.

▪ Breathe regularly and close your eyes. Tune in to each of your other senses, noticing all the sounds you hear, odors or fragrances, flavors on your tongue, and all the textures and temperatures your skin is experiencing.

▪ Bring your legs together and your arms over your head. Breathe in, and on the exhale, become as long and large as you can, from the tips of your fingers to your toes. Breathe and stretch three times. Feel your length.

- Slowly turn over onto your belly and stretch as long as you can. Breathe and relax, arms to your sides and head turned to one side.

- Come onto your knees, stretch arms high, then slowly stretch them in front of you until your forehead touches the floor. Breathe and relax, rocking gently to and fro.

- Moving like a ballerina, stand. Place your feet parallel, arms to sides, then straighten your spine, elongating your body fully from the crown of your head to the soles of your feet. Feel your connection to the Earth, reaching to the heavens. Breathe and smile three times.

- Spread your legs and arms wide, taking up as much space as you can. Breathe and smile. Feel your powerful body.

Connecting to your history—
Try this more than once.

- Now, go to your "keeper" places; select some items from your childhood. Hold them close, close your eyes, sniff, touch, and remember.

- Choose one item that particularly touches your emotions. Visit it with all your senses and allow yourself to go back. Close your eyes for awhile as you hold onto the thread of your innocence. Allow emotions to flood your being.

- Write, draw, or tell this story to someone you trust, real or imaginary.

- What are the threads of your innocent childhood that are woven into your adult self?

- Name the most powerful threads which support your being. Begin to imagine how you can transform the painful tears or knots into strong, resilient aspects of your life design. Breathe into this vision, allowing it to become clear.

Expanding—
Select an activity each week this month.

- Turn your attention to people in your immediate environment. Who do you know that is struggling with conditions beyond his or her control? Listen to this person; find out what steps you can help them take toward their empowerment. Take one step with them today, another tomorrow, and another.

- Explore alternative clothing manufacturers who pay living wages, only employing union workers. The Clean Clothes Connection publishes a list. Next time you buy,

Fibre crafts from women's sewing cooperatives in Peru and Guatemala are available online.

find out about the human behind the garment and choose accordingly.

- Read the article "The Global Cooperative Campaign Against Poverty," online at www.ica.coop/outofpoverty. It explains the cooperative movement as well as fair-trade practices. Research at least one women's cooperative movement in a developing country. What is your response? With whom will you share this awareness? How can you support the efforts of these women?

- Learn about the history of textiles from the perspective of the weavers of India. Learn also about the ways in which England's textile industry impacted cotton production in Africa and the United States.

POWER AND INNOCENCE PROJECT

FINGER CROCHETING

Abbie encircled by her finger-crocheted, portable labyrinth.

Katie provided this story and project about her seven-year-old grandson, Jack—a project later completed by one of my own grandchildren.

• • •

"I'll never be bored again!" said Jack. He watched in amazement as Katie showed him how to finger crochet a yarn chain. He thought it was almost magical to be able to create something out of practically nothing.

She sent him home with a bright blue skein of yarn. He was so taken with his new skill that the next time Katie saw him, he proudly showed her the chain he had made. It stretched out the length of his room and back again! Enthusiastically he rattled off his plans for making it into a rug, placemat, or whatever.

• • •

Here is the project that so enthralled innocent Jack and provided a surge of power. As you experience the meditative aspect of this simple project, focus on innocence—yours and others. Then, experience your power as you transform your work into something strong and useful!

You will need

- One ball of yarn in any color or fibre type desired.
- The innocence of a child, and/or a child with whom to work; eager and willing hands.

The process

- Begin by tying a slip knot with five or six inches left hanging loosely, as a tail.
- Loosen the opening of the slip knot enough to insert both thumb and first finger.
- Pinch the yarn between thumb and first finger, pulling a new loop through the first loop. Pull on this until the first loop is fairly snug around it.
- Repeat this process of pulling new loops through the previous loops, then tightening up the slack, until you have a chain as long as you wish.
- Secure the end by cutting the yarn and pulling the tail through the last loop.
- This chain can now be made into all sorts of creations, as Jack demonstrated. Let your innocent child imagine and produce something original! You might even consider weaving enough chain to create a portable labyrinth.

HOOKS AND NEEDLES AT SCHOOL

No, we are not talking about drug use! Instead, this is about the many innovative programs employing crochet hooks, knitting and sewing needles in elementary schools. Teachers and counselors attest to a variety of benefits to students and others. Included among the benefits are enhanced math skills, boosted self-esteem, more focused attention, fine motor coordination, and developed social skills.

Math requirements for fibre projects are perhaps surprising, but ask a quilter and you will hear about not only simple stitch counting, but about subtraction, multiplication, division, figuring fractions, and the geometry of pattern. One quilter I met had color-coded the tiny squares of solved Sudoku puzzles and created a quilt using these patterns. Amazing to me! So, kids can learn to count stitches, increase or decrease, and understand pattern and ratio in creating a fibre project.

With guidance, even kindergartners can learn simple fibre arts. In northern Thailand, we watched elders teach village boys and girls to weave the pattern of their tribe, the Akha.

Much more happens when kids pick up needles and hooks to create. The activity requires focused attention. For many children, this is challenging in verbal or auditory learning, but becomes possible when tactile and kinesthetic senses are involved. Once focused, there is a meditative relaxation to the activity; this quiet time of engagement offers important settling for extremely active children.

Helping one another, watching the projects of others as they evolve, and sharing tools, materials, and techniques are avenues for developing social skills. In some cases, the scarves, mittens, or small blankets created are donated to charity projects. What a fabulous way for kids to learn the deep joy of compassion and contribution!

Amelia shared the story of her niece bursting in the door after school, interrupting the adult conversation to announce, "I finished my hat and it fits just right! Look!" Wearing the hat was a classmate, bald from the chemotherapy she was enduring.

Perhaps the most valuable gift of fibre work in the school setting is the sense of competence each child feels in creating something useful and/or beautiful that did not previously exist. To choose a project, selecting colors and yarns, taps the child's creativity; to actually create the imagined item is cause for great exclamation. In the process, they can also learn to rip out and redo in order to accomplish their goal. Children who develop a sense of competence are more likely to succeed in school and in life.

Pick up those hooks and needles, kids, and help create a soulful world!

Chapter 4

THREADS OF IDENTITY

Muslim Prayer for Peace

In the name of Allah, the beneficent, the merciful.

Praise be to the Lord of the Universe who has created us and

made us into tribes and nations, that we may know each other,

not that we may despise each other.

If the enemy incline towards peace,

do thou also incline towards peace,

And trust in God,

for the Lord is the one that heareth and knoweth all things.

And the servants of God, Most Gracious, are those

who walk on the Earth in humility,

And when we address them, we say "peace."

Banjara women of India, in their traditional dress

THREADS OF IDENTITY

Team uniforms are well-known threads of identity in the world of sports. These high school tennis players wear the royal blue jerseys of their team, the Vikings.

• • •

Gangs in the United States emerged initially along ethnic lines, as groups of immigrants competed for jobs, territory, and status. Gang identity began to include clothing, called "colors." Treatment programs offer trade-ins, providing jackets in neutral colors.

• • •

"Chain Gangs" is a term sometimes employed by groups of knitters and crocheters who come together through their fibre arts to create positive contributions.

• • •

Go online to check out Wool and the Gang, a company and a family gang of knitters, from age seven to 77. This family group, that has bonded through knitting, works with indigenous people in Peru.

The elderly woman was amazed at the six-year-old boy on the teeter-totter rattling off the names of the U.S. presidents, in order.
"How do you know so much?" she asked.
"I'm smart! I'm a Peterson!" was the small fellow's enthusiastic response.

Passing the football field by the school near her office late on a crisp fall day, Anna and I hear the cheerleaders shouting, "We are the Tigers, the mighty, mighty Tigers!" Peering over the fence, we see five young women in gold and black striped sweaters roaring out to the world, a single male among them. We watch, then continue our walk through swishing autumn leaves, discussing the challenge the young man must face to identify with the stereotypically feminine role of cheerleader while his buddies are largely on the team.

Anna, a therapist with three teenagers of her own, knows well the challenges of adolescent identity formation; she conducts a knitting therapy group for teens at this school, often with a waiting list.

"Everyone needs a sense of belonging—to something or someone where they are accepted and valued and validated. It's the power of gangs!" Anna says.

"In the group, while we knit, these young people talk about how hard it is to fit in, to feel like they are worthwhile. High schools are notorious for their cliques. It is difficult for anyone who doesn't identify clearly with a group. The knitting not only serves as a vehicle to right-brain activity and provides a sense of competence, but also gives them a sense of belonging.

"Everyone first knits a rainbow bandana that they wear throughout our meetings and elsewhere, if they wish. It's an easy way to learn to knit. And, the finished bandana is their mark of membership—which they seem to love."

"But, how do you get these kids to come to your group?" I ask.

"Most are referred by school counselors," Anna tells me. "They have seen their pain as they sit alone at lunch. Or, the kids come in to talk to the counselors

The Gulabi Gang in India does not refer to themselves as a gang in "the usual sense of the term." This group of women call themselves a gang for justice, taking out retribution upon men who abuse women. They say that they wear pink because "it is the color of life."

about being bullied or teased. They feel like they are real misfits. Loners. And it hurts. Many come to my group tentatively, but they seem drawn to the focus on knitting rather than on therapy. We have soft drinks and hang out a bit, with no demands to talk. It's a sort of buffer. They can focus on creating something rather than on their sense of loneliness." Anna pauses, then smiles. "It's really fun to see them get started. Pretty soon they are showing off their knitting and they are talking like mad about being misfits. Yet, they no longer are! I love watching the transformation."

We arrive at the brick library, covered with the deep burgundy ivy of fall, where Ying, a young Hmong college student, has agreed to talk to a small group about her family and life events before coming to the United States. She participated in Anna's knitting group during her high school years. Ying surprises us by appearing in a very ornate traditional Hmong ceremonial dress in vivid contrasts of pinks, yellows, greens; her movement jingles the attached silver coins and metallic adornment. She describes the history sewn into her skirt: layers of batik, embroidery, and pleating, "a way to preserve my life in Laos." Ying explains that this is a ceremonial costume sewn for the celebration of the New Year, the most festive of Hmong occasions.

She tells us that women in her culture are identified by their sewing skill; expected to sew everyday clothing for their families as well as elaborate ceremonial

Ying and friend in traditional attire of Laotian Hmong

In their embroidered *huipiles*, Manuela and Alyssa express their Mayan identity in the Yucatan.

gowns. Most women take great pride in their needlework. It is a way to remain Hmong even while adapting to the U.S. culture.

At a very early age, a young girl in Laos would learn to sew under the guidance of her mother and grandmother. Gender divisions were pronounced. A girl's sewing proficiency decided her eligibility for marriage, even if she was very young. She remained ineligible if she did not master the art. "Yikes! I'd never be eligible!" I think to myself.

Anna asks Ying about the transition she and her family have had to make in leaving Laos and settling in the United States. Ying explains that, though the new culture was very difficult at first, it has been easier for her, as a younger person, than for her parents. She describes a group of older Hmong women gathering to stitch their traditional needlework, *paj ntaub*, making burial garments for themselves. The group gathered to practice the needlework, but it became a support group for these displaced women. They found a sense of belonging in the process, "just as we did in your knitting group, Anna," Ying says with gratitude. She intends to continue her needlework although she mostly wears Western clothing now. "I want to hand it down to my daughter someday, so there is still a piece of Laos living on. It is who we are."

Indeed, "who we are." Identity is defined in part through the fibre work of cultures.

I invite Ying and Anna to our church next week when my friend Jan and I will be sharing our experience of the indigenous communities in Chiapas, Mexico, and our batik experience on a Yucatan beach.

Ying and Anna sit in the front row on Sunday as we begin our story. Latin music provides ambiance, while the church hosts the pleasant aromas of the many dishes warming for our follow-up potluck.

Jan and I begin, soon losing ourselves in the reverie. Manuela, Alyssa, Angelina, Juanita, Nicolina. Names of Mayan women Jan and I met during our two weeks in Mexico, both on the Yucatan Peninsula and in Chiapas—women whose identity is expressed in their hand-embroidered *huipiles*.

As often is the case these days, Manuela and Alyssa

The orange and red stripes of Amatenango

ern garb has taken place. Our initial introduction to the marks of identity in this indigenous community occurred at an ecumenical mass conducted by the local priest and our protestant minister.

As the pure voices of these small, gentle people rose in song, we looked out to the right at a sea of white shawls draped over the heads and shoulders of the women. White-shirted men filled the pews to the left. Only afterwards, when we gathered for reflection group, shawls absent, did we see the striking red and orange bands that comprise the bodice of the Amatenango *huipil,* accented by plaid turbans and dark plaid skirts.

The reflection group included intergenerational members of the parish, from babies to elderly folks. We discussed, through interpreters of Tzotzil, our uniqueness and commonalities. Like Alyssa and Manuela, the women were excited to tell us about their *huipiles,* exuding pride in their embroidery skills and their identity.

A woman in Amatenango typically owns two *huipiles,* each taking about three weeks of intense all-day embroidery to create. One is kept especially for Sundays and celebrations. The other is for everyday wear, worn while throwing pottery, grinding corn, gathering wood, and other labors necessary to the subsistence life of this economically challenged region.

The women poured mugs of thick rich chocolate for us to drink. We became more comfortable and continued to talk, needing less and less interpretation. Sisters Angelina and Nicolina wore the same *huipil* as their mother, with one exception: vertical stripes in bright colors decorate the broad bands of red and orange brocade on the younger women, but their mother's bands stretch uninterrupted. Angelina's preteen daughter, Juanita, wore a ruffled white blouse decorated with flowers.

When I asked the significance of the colorful stripes and the absence of it on some, the women giggled. The difference in the *huipiles* indicates reproductive status: before menarche, young girls do not wear the *huipil;* following menopause, the colorful stripes are removed. Not only the community, but even one's age

were dressed in ordinary Western garb for most of the week we shared with them at the workshop on the beach: jeans or shorts, t-shirts. But on the last night, when the smells of the traditional Mayan meal lured us early to the outdoor table, Manuela and Alyssa appeared, dark eyes twinkling, in their striking dresses of white cotton with vibrant flowers embroidered on the bodice and skirt.

The women spoke proudly of their work and their Mayan identity. The *huipiles* deepened our appreciation for the rich lime soup and corn pudding wrapped in banana leaves, the warm salt breeze and rhythmic undulations of the Caribbean enveloping us in an ancient culture.

In Amatenango, Chiapas, no such defection to West-

This *huipil* hangs in honor of those killed in a nonviolent, resistance movement in Chiapas, Mexico, in 1997.

and stage of life are visible in the blouse each woman stitches.

Protective of their identity and their impeccable needlework, the women of Amatenango have elected not to sell these blouses to outsiders. Other communities have chosen to do so, providing much-needed income. Angelina and Nicolina prefer to earn income through their pottery rather than weakening the sense of identity they exercise by the exclusive right to wear their specific *huipil*.

Later, we visited a wall in a small chapel where hangs a very special *huipil* intended to identify not only a community, but a cause, stitched in memory of 45 women, children, and men massacred in Acteal in December 1997. These people were members of a nonviolent resistance movement known as *Las Abejas,* The Bees.

Our interpreter told us the very moving story of the cause and of the massacre. As "bees," the group used "stingers" to name injustice, moved from village to village informing workers, and served the "queen," their organization. Associated with a group committed to self-defense of their communities, the *Zapatistas, Las Abejas* became the target of a paramilitary attack in spite of being pacifist.

Assassins opened fire on the small religious group while they were praying in their church, continuing to pick them off if they moved, for several hours. The dead included 14 children under age 10, five teenagers, four pregnant women, and 21 other adults. Community members have hung this *huipil* in a place of honor, with the identities of the victims printed and framed beneath it. We became silent in sadness.

Though these are powerful representations of identity through wearable art, in the several other indigenous communities we visited, the *huipil* was less obvious. Many of the women, especially younger ones hoping to gain acceptance in the larger society, opted not to wear them. There certainly remains a sense of identity, however, in the floral designs adorning many blouses and the broadband dark skirts nearly everyone wore. The vibrant colors of the shawls in which most women wrapped themselves also identified their creative nature.

Jan and I conclude our sharing with an invitation to continue discussion downstairs while we enjoy the feast. Several choir members pause to remove their robes. Our minister does the same. Now their identity melds with the rest.

"Think about the fibre creations that define membership," Anna begins. She gobbles a bite of chicken mole. "Betsy Ross stitched the first U.S. flag. Flags represent our identity as citizens of specific nations.

"And uniforms! Uniforms define membership—occupations, bands, armies, choirs, even prisoners."

"Yes, and think about the way specific fibre creations are associated with countries even though they aren't worn as badges of membership—Turkish socks, Norwegian sweaters, the blankets of the Navajo weavers," Ying adds. "All of these are indications of belonging."

"Plus, the guilds formed around specific fibre arts offer instant belonging to newcomers. Weavers, spinners, quilters—all have guilds that meet regularly. So if you are new to an area, you find a group of people with a common love," Jan points out.

I pause, remembering a profoundly moving film, *Water*, about India's widows who live as outcasts, marked by shorn hair, a smear on their face, and the swaddling wrap of cream-colored fabric.

"Membership is not always chosen. Identification with some groups is not necessarily desired. Sameness removes individuality. I understand that some women in the Middle East are protesting the wearing of the *burqa* for that very reason," I say.

Talk continues in small groups as the meal is consumed. People begin to leave. We linger, cleaning up and distributing the leftovers. Finally, only Anna and I remain. We are reluctant to part. On the way to our cars, I inquire about the gender makeup of Anna's group. She confirms that only an occasional male participates.

"Stereotypes are hard to break. Belonging is an important human need, but it also can restrict our identity," Anna states.

This reminds me of my husband's courage to step out of the restrictions of gender roles, and of courageous others

The *huipil* and the *burqa* define identity within culture.

My husband, Bob, learned to sew at age 10. He now enjoys crafting furniture, toys, and stained-glass works.

who have claimed their right to belong and to remain unique.

Bob is, at first gloss, a typical male in our U.S. culture. A craftsman of fine quality wood creations, including furniture with a reputation for sturdy, enduring beauty, Bob enjoys tearing apart an old building or dock, board by board, nail by nail; there is little he will not tackle, from electrical wiring to plumbing to roofing. His favorite clothes are well-weathered jeans and a paint-speckled sweatshirt.

Bob also expresses his feminine aspect. He makes sweet wooden toys and children's furniture. Lanterns, picture frames, computer desks, entertainment centers have all taken form under his creative hand. Every holiday season, he designs and makes 100 stained-glass angels which become gifts to friends, family, and people around the community who have touched his heart during the year.

We have been married for two-thirds of our lives. I moved onto his street near the end of high school; we attended college while living in our parents' homes. I proudly bought myself a new coat from money earned working to pay tuition. Classes and work, though, left

"...one can undertake any voyage if the destination is home.... When a place to belong is assured, the adventure of growth can begin with great promise."
—John O'Donohue

little time to do the necessary shortening of the hem.

One night Bob walked down to my parents' home and asked for my new coat; I'm sure my parents were perplexed. He took it to his house, put it on his younger sister who was about my height, pinned it to a reasonable length, and neatly sewed that hem in place. I came home from work that night to a new coat, ready to wear.

After losing his dad in a plane crash, eight-year-old Bob was nurtured by the women in his life; a favorite aunt offered to make him a special shirt if he first accomplished one on his own. He found a checkered cotton fabric; his mom purchased it for him and helped him get started. Though it was too small to wear by the time he enlisted help from a family friend to make the button holes, he did accomplish the task. I am awed by that endeavor. What 10-year-old male would pay attention to the beauty of a particular fabric, much less create a garment from it? What wonderful wisdom from the women in his life—aunt, mother, friend—to encourage him to sew.

"Anna, it seems to me that identity involves belonging as well as the strength to break away when belonging impedes our fullness," I say now. "It is remarkable to me that, as we speak, Oprah is delivering a eulogy at the memorial for Coretta Scott King, and just months ago, Rosa Parks was the first woman to lie in state in the capitol rotunda. These women refused to be limited by gender, class, race, or glass ceilings. Their individual identity took precedence over their membership in categories. Their belonging now is to the human race."

Anna agrees, "It certainly is a complex issue, how we conceptualize ourselves; but, right now the family to which I belong is probably wondering where I am. I need to get home so I have some time with the kids before the weekend is over. Enjoy your day!"

I head home, determined to shorten my own jeans.

THREADS FOR THOUGHT

•We develop an evolving self-concept, a sense of who we are as differentiated from others, in early childhood. This gradually becomes our individual identity, our sense of "Me."

•We also develop a sense of "Not-Me," those characteristics that we deny or reject about ourselves. Carl Jung called this sense the "Shadow." Making peace with our shadow helps us become more fully functioning human beings.

•This self-concept is shaped by our interactions with significant others in our lives in an ever-widening sphere.

•Our sense of self influences, and is influenced by, our families, schools, religious affiliations, communities, cultural expectations, and nationalities. Whether we feel accepted or rejected is the interaction between these influences and our way of being.

•Social identity is our sense of self, reflected by our identification with membership in specific groups.

•Emile Durkheim's research on suicide indicates that this sense of social identity is critical to our individual well-being.

•Strong identification with groups, denial of shadow aspects, and a sense of moral rightness can lead to feuding families, religious fanaticism, and nation-building.

•A superordinate goal, one that requires the pooling of resources of differing factions, leads to cooperative collaboration. How will our lives be different when our shared goal of "peace on Earth" prevails?

•How will our lives be different when we all identify ourselves as members of the family of humankind and weave a flag of many colors, textures, designs, and fibres?

•How will our lives be different when we identify the Earth's resources and creatures as part of our shared culture?

ACTIVITIES • IDs, PLEASE

"Peace in one's self will bring about peace in one's community, in the world."
—Thich Nhat Hanh

These activities are designed to focus on ways in which our sense of identity forms and informs our interactions with the world, and how we can limit or expand our concepts of others through group membership.

Festivals, parades, and market days bring out an exquisite range of traditional clothing. These women are wearing folk costumes of a region in Sardinia.

Connecting within—
Breathe and connect daily.

- Begin with some deep belly breaths, centering yourself and focusing inward.

- Whisper your full name three times and imagine your soul slipping into a little pocket right behind your heart.

- Close your eyes and let an image of yourself as a small child form in your mind. Spend a little time with her, then allow the image to mature a few years. Progress into your teen self, and then adulthood.

- On a large sheet of paper, place the words, "I am" in the center. Without censorship, write quickly in a web around these words, descriptive phrases about yourself. Continue until you feel completely emptied.

- Sit back from this web of identity and reflect on all the threads you have spun. The statements you have listed reflect your self-concept.

- Look for common themes and combine those that go together. These "I am…" statements are the beliefs you have formed about yourself.

- Ask yourself the source of these beliefs about yourself— parental messages, experiences, religious dogma?

- Decide which are alterable and which are fixed.

- Choose one fixed quality and make a positive statement about that.

- Choose one alterable quality and set a goal for change.

Connecting interpersonally—
Try one of these each week this month.

- Now turn your attention outside of yourself. Think about categories in which we tend to define others. Think about your value judgments regarding these categories (boxes).

- Identify one person that you have avoided because you have judged their membership in some category. Make contact with that person. Learn his or her name. Find out about his or her life. Challenge yourself to re-evaluate your judgment.

- Is there a group from which you have been denied membership? What feelings do you experience about this group? How can this help you understand the rage of oppressed, excluded groups?

- Explore cultures with which you are unfamiliar. Learn as much as you can about the uniqueness of each culture.

- Research the fibre arts of one culture on each continent!

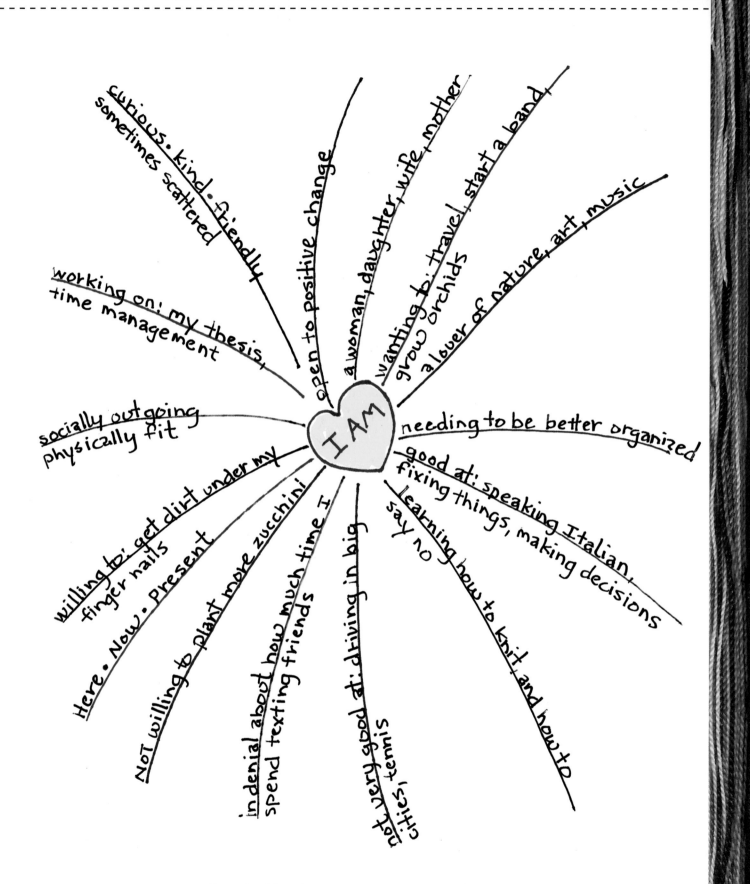

Example of "I am" writing activity, described on facing page

PROJECT • CRESTS

In the tradition of Celtic crests, I made this personal crest, to represent myself in the context of family.

The Celts were one of many traditions capturing their identity through symbols that were designed on a crest, then applied to clothing, dishes, and shields. This project is to develop your own symbolic crest—with permeable membranes!

You will need
- A background piece of light or white fabric, about 12" x 18"—preferably cotton or cotton blend.

The process
- Draw a crest (shaped like a shield, a heart, a circle) approximately the size of your white cotton fabric on a piece of paper; use this as your pattern to cut the white cotton into this shape.

- Draw light pencil lines dividing the shape into six sections. Stitch yarns or cord along these lines to define the sections. Leave a small unstitched area at the outer edge without a divider (permeable membrane).

- Now, think of the ways you defined yourself in the activities above. Think of one section of your crest as your individual identity. Select something simple and symbolic to represent that, such as your initials. Sketch this, then color it in using fabric crayons, fabric markers, or fabric paints.

- Do the same with the remaining sections representing your family identity, your occupational identity, your national identity, and the remaining two sections representing other significant group memberships with which you identify.

- When your sections are all colored with symbols, embroider the aspects you want to stand out, using simple chain stitches or more elaborate stitches.

- Finally, stitch a border around the entire crest on the background fabric, leaving an opening to allow the freedom to step beyond these boundaries.

- Hang this on your closet door to remind yourself each day that you belong to the family of humankind with all its rights and responsibilities!

REPEATING PATTERNS • FRACTALS

Repeating patterns, like frost on this window, show up in our lives and relationships.

Patterns are essential to fibre workers. They are not only the templates from which garments and textiles are created, but are a part of the creation itself, in the pattern of the threads, the colors, the design. Patterns surround us in nature, but we seldom notice. Patterns in our behavior can assist or restrict our ability to create soulful, peaceful lives.

Pause now to look at the veins in your hands. Then the leafless branches of a large deciduous tree. A topographical map of a river delta. Can you see the common pattern? Can you also see how the pattern within each repeats in ever smaller versions? These irregular repeating patterns in nature are the stuff of fractal geometry. Fascinating! They offer tremendous inspiration for design and texture in textiles.

My friend Donna loved every aspect of sewing. She considered it a perfect day when she could head for her favorite fabric store, pore through the pattern books selecting just the right look, sensuously examine fabrics for the desired texture, color, design, then complete this first phase by choosing buttons, threads, and other suggested notions. What amazed me is that she also loved going home to fit, press, and trim the pattern. Too tedious for me! Good preparation, though, is key to successful outcome in sewing as well as in many other domains. Working consciously with patterns determines the outcome. (This explains my dissatisfaction with the sewing I have attempted!)

Repeating patterns in our lives show up especially in our relationships. We may ponder the tendency, for instance, of repeatedly choosing an abusive partner. Finally leaving one bad relationship, many often enter another similarly abusive one. We wonder aloud why this person did not recognize that this choice was simply repeating the previous one. Until we bring to conscious awareness our behavioral patterns, they will operate at an unconscious level.

How conscious are we of the repeating patterns in our lives? Are they useful templates that guide us, or have they become so habituated that they restrict the outcomes we seek? We can make conscious our patterns by observing ourselves, identifying patterns needing change, then patiently taking all the slow, tedious steps in preparation for the desired outcome.

Chapter 5

BRAIDING
INTIMATE CORDS

Sikh Prayer for Peace
God adjudges us according to our deeds,
not the coat that we wear: that Truth is above everything,
but higher still is truthful living.
Know that we attaineth God when we loveth,
and only that victory endures
in consequence of which no one is defeated.

Generations of cords and scarves, bonded in braids

BRAIDING INTIMATE CORDS

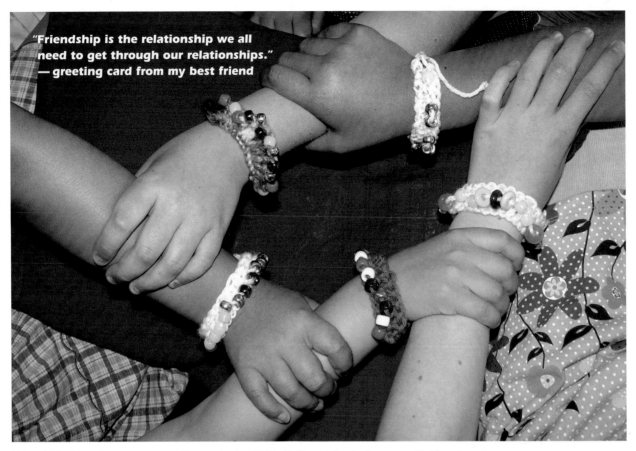

"Friendship is the relationship we all need to get through our relationships."
— greeting card from my best friend

Friendship bracelets are among the projects at Kids Knitwork in Burlingame, California.

arie and I are in a fibre artists' heaven —the scarf department of an exclusive upscale shop on a corner frequented by the Aunt Anns of the world. She is intent on splurging on one very special scarf to adorn a plain dress she sewed for her stepson's wedding and has asked me to help her with the selection.

Honestly, her voice becomes husky and she sounds orgasmic as she strokes one particularly smooth, sleek silk in deep rich colors that seduces one longingly into its fibres. I hush her regretfully, reminding her that we are in public!

"I know," she exclaims, "but don't you just want to merge with it, explore it languorously, and let it drape your naked body?"

More reserved, I say, "No," and move to another rack, less sensuous.

But, truth is, fibres are sensuous, and fibre arts create intimate connections. Just as the artists twist and weave and entwine individual threads and yarns into forever-joined fabrics and garments, the lives of the artists themselves are entwined and forever joined into new creations.

Our culture is one that stresses autonomy, not intimacy. Yet we have a longing to know and to be known. So often, sex is mistakenly defined as intimacy, but emotional intimacy is at least as important to humans as sexual intimacy. Marie and I discuss the difference between intimacy and sex, lamenting the skewed attitudes in our culture of alienation. Marie describes sex in America as another spectator sport, focused on performance rather than sensuous experiencing. "That's why," she states, "I'd rather be intimate with a scarf than a person."

Over lunch—her lustful purchase clutched possessively in a very classy bag—Marie and I talk about my beloved best friend, Donna, who sewed for me as an expression of our deep friendship. We met as graduate students sitting across from one another on the grass in a class on group dynamics. Donna later told me that she thought I was either a nun or an accountant because of my tightly buttoned blouse with a proper blue jacket. Her strapless sundress and dangling earrings appealed to me immediately. We had coffee afterward and began a quarter-century friendship.

Donna wisely set out to loosen up my rigid demeanor by creating bold, fluid outfits for me, especially if I were giving a presentation.

I laughingly tell Marie about the hours we would spend, imagining the outfit I wanted, then shopping for pattern, fabric, and notions.

Always, we would stop for a latte, over which we would review the image, caress the fabric, and plan the process. Often, I would spend the night at her house; we'd trim the pattern and then fit it. Believe me, Donna was the only woman who touched my body, knew my hip size, and was allowed a guffaw without incurring my wrath!

True intimacy occurred during these projects because we would spend focused time with each other, talking, sharing our essential selves, sometimes crying, frequently laughing and occasionally fighting. "That," I say to Marie, "is the true test of intimacy… to be safe enough to have great fights and to trust that the relationship will survive!"

"That's a huge key to developing true intimacy," says Marie. "Conflict is inevitable, but we don't handle it well. Either we 'stuff' our feelings and opinions, or we seem to lash out at others. Trust in a relationship, especially when there is conflict, is hard. You have to trust in yourself before you can trust another. I have trouble letting someone see my negative side. I want them to see only the part of me that's nice."

"Is that why you are always crocheting slippers and booties and sweet things for all of us? You are too nice

My friendship with Donna, at right, grew during the hours she spent sewing clothes for me.

for your own good! When do you let yourself be angry or ask for something for yourself?"

"Well, I am working on it. That's why I bought the scarf instead of giving the money to the kids for the wedding. I think it came from having to be nice when I was a kid because of my mom's drinking. If I did nice things for her, I felt loved."

We discuss the many ways we tend to defer to others in order to feel loved and to avoid conflict. I tell Marie about Caroline Myss's encouragement to view those who offer us our greatest challenges as special angels who are helping us to learn our most important soul lessons.

Just then another friend walks by; we beckon her in and fill her in on our conversation topic of "intimacy and scarves."

"Oh," Judie says, "I have an intimate scarf story to tell you—about my mother! Want to hear it?"

She needn't ask.

Judie describes a floral silk scarf that her mother wore frequently when she was growing up, and nearly constantly after her father died. Finally daring to ask where it came from, her mother simply replied, "A friend." Judie understood that she would hear no more from her mother about that friend, but also knew there was a story behind this scarf.

After her mother's death some years later, Judie asked her aunt, who was her mother's closest sister, about the scarf. Her aunt told her about a male friend who had been her mother's constant companion while Judie's father was off to war. This friend gave Judie's mother the scarf the week before her father's return; they never saw one another again.

"A friend may well be reckoned the masterpiece of nature."
—Ralph Waldo Emerson

• • •

Handmade friendship bracelets, such as the Peruvian bracelets above, have been a popular gift among young girls. Traditionally they are worn until the threads weaken and the bracelets fall off naturally.

• • •

Most styles of friendship bracelets are created using techniques of macramé, a centuries-old form of creative knot-tying that was widely popular in the 1970s.

• • •

Early sailors were known for transforming functional, nautical knots into elaborate coverings for knife handles and bottles. Macramé has also appeared on the red carpet, in friendship bracelets worn by celebrities.

But the scarf was with her, intimately caressing her neck, shoulders, and breasts, for the rest of her life. Now Judie has the scarf and intends to frame it.

"Wow, you seem very accepting, Judie," I acknowledge.

"Well, you know the idea of casting the first stone," she replies.

Suddenly Marie exclaims, "Let's call Amelia and get her over here! She has been grieving in silence and it is time for her to trust us with her grief about this divorce thing." She dials and a soggy Amelia answers, obviously not set for coming out to join us. "Then we'll be over in about a half hour," Marie says powerfully. "Jump in the shower and break out that boxed wine you've been saving for your best friends!"

I feel hesitant, knowing how I like my solitude when I am distressed, but Judie agrees with Marie and the three of us gather our treasures. Judie calls to let her partner know she will be home late. Marie and I had already made that clear.

Indeed, Amelia was freshly showered, hair still damp, and seemed to be touched by our caring. Instead of the boxed wine, she had opened a good bottle of merlot and had her delicate hand-painted glasses ready. We sit in her sun porch on huge pillows she had covered with her needle-felted designs. She lights orange-scented candles and puts on the soundtrack from *Brokeback Mountain*. The music is haunting and tugs at the threads of sadness in each of our intimate lives.

Our now animated conversation turns to "scarves we have known" and we share stories of secret loves and wounded hearts and dreams continuing…and we know that what we are doing is deepening an intimate friendship.

It is Judie who says, "Amelia, we have been sharing our deepest longings and pains, but you have not yet talked about Kurt wanting a divorce. Do you not trust us?"

"It's not you I don't trust! It's myself. If I start to talk about it, I know I will go on and on and I'll cry and then I'll be embarrassed. I can only hold myself together if I don't talk about it."

"Well, of course you will cry and cry. Isn't that what we have tears for? And, we need to go over and over the events of our lives that have shocked or hurt or scared us. It's how we come to terms with them eventually. That's why women are so good for one another. We are good at talking and listening and processing endlessly. And, we know how to cry and we know when it's time to let somebody else cry without trying to comfort them. My therapist once said to me as I began to stifle my sobs, 'Let me hear your sound!'"

Before I can say more, Amelia is sobbing in great waves. We surround her and just let her cry and cry and cry. When her sobs begin to ebb, Marie picks up a soft crocheted shawl from her couch and gently wraps Amelia's drooping shoulders. Judie begins to hum soft lullabies, and before long, Marie and I join in as we cradle and rock our hurting friend in a chrysalis of tender fibres. Finally, Amelia begins to talk and everything pours forth.

Kurt had been having an affair with his teaching partner and they had both decided to end their marriages to be together. Amelia questions herself endlessly, rages about Kurt, rages about "the bitch," and spirals back to tears again.

She cries about all she had given up for the marriage. "I didn't even go to church because Kurt didn't want to," she sobs. "And I lived in the city instead of the woods I loved because he preferred sidewalks!"

Well after midnight, we decide that going home is useless. After calling partners, we pop in a frozen pizza and talk until nearly dawn. In the process, we strengthen the fibres of our friendship as we let down the barriers that we imagine separating us from one another.

The next morning, this puffy-eyed, sleep-deprived little group stirs from makeshift nests of slumber to discover Amelia in the kitchen, humming as she sits with aromatic fresh coffee, working on the needle-felting project she had started at our last retreat.

After a long night of tears, Amelia emerged with a completed needlework that symbolized her freedom.

She grins as we shuffle in, then holds up her nearly finished project; we let out synchronized giggles when we see the colorful fibre portrait of an angel soaring the heavens, looking a bit like Amelia—a symbol of freedom flying across the deep purple, wool sky.

Thanks, you guys!" says Amelia as she gets up to embrace the three of us in a group hug. "I needed a purging cry to really feel the surge of freedom that I have been aching for. Last night was that release and

• • •

Trying to come to terms with loss often requires repeated review of the events—it is as though we are trying to create a space for the reality. Women often fear that this will tire others and then deny themselves the process.

• • •

Women have been socialized to deny anger while men have been socialized to deny fears and sadness. We need both in order to have a full range of emotional expression.

• • •

Gloria Steinem defines a codependent as "a well-socialized woman." But, the impact of addictions and other unhealthy dynamics in families does contribute to a pattern of seeking love by constantly giving and doing for others, to the neglect of self.

Carol Gilligan's landmark study of gender differences in play suggests that, when there is conflict, girls will forfeit the game rather than the relationship.

• • •

The game of Korfbol was specifically designed to be played by mixed teams of men and women.

today I feel like I am ready to soar! Our group is the warp through which I am able to weave my grief. I am so grateful."

We each wipe a tired tear as we pour ourselves some coffee and launch into more life processing. We know that Amelia has lots more grieving to do before she really soars, but we also know that she is on her way. And, we know that each of us would receive the same support and encouragement from our group that Amelia is experiencing in her healing process.

Quilters, spinners, seamstresses work together and share souls in the process.

Marcy describes her quilting group as her grief therapy following the death of her husband; Mary tells how lonely she was following a cross-country move, until she joined the local weavers' guild and felt immediately at home; Jacqui declares that her annual "sewers" retreat is her survival; Patrice emotionally talks of her spinning circle as "my other family—the one that truly accepts me for who I am."

Fibre artists come together to share their passion and their deepest, most authentic selves. Everyone is enriched and health is enhanced.

Fibre arts not only give people a sense of belonging to a group, but often are the connectors of lives that become deeply entwined and allow one another to know and be known and accepted, with warts and beauty marks. As we talk and share more stories, I am reminded of the women of Java in their batik circles and of our own group that gathers, sometimes around fibre arts as we did on our recent retreat.

In hunter-gatherer societies of long ago, women gathered not only roots and seeds and fibres, but gathered communally to process them. Traditionally the "tenders of the hearth," women naturally come together in community to teach and share and learn. In so doing, their individual fibres are connected and souls are merged.

Amelia lends me some fleece fabric, bits of dyed wool, a ratcheted needle, and a piece of foam, then teaches me the basics of needle felting. Everything I see on the way home becomes a source of inspiration; I can't wait to try capturing these scenes.

THREADS FOR THOUGHT

•Our need to bond with others begins in infancy, perhaps in utero; Harry Harlow's famous monkey experiments indicate that mammals seek comfort in the softness of another rather than simply seeking a food supply.

•Ashley Montagu stresses the critical role of nurturing touch for human well-being, not just in infancy, but throughout our lifetime.

•Orphaned babies in France "failed to thrive" if given only food, water, and minimal hygiene; human attention and touch were as essential to the babies' development as the basic needs.

•Oxytocin is a hormone that plays a major role in giving birth, in lactation, and in sexual orgasm. A 1999 study at the University of California, San Francisco, indicates that oxytocin may also impact our ability to bond in close personal relationships.

•Emotional expression is a key factor in the development of intimate relationships. Robert Sternberg's triangular theory describes passion, intimacy, and commitment as the tripod essential to enduring, "consummate love."

•Candace Pert, author of *Molecules of Emotion*, identifies sites throughout the body containing

Traditional braids worn in Guatemala

receptors to peptides that are released with the experience of strong emotion. Pert cites evidence that unexpressed emotion causes illness.

•One indicator of anorexia bulimia, a common eating disorder prevalent among women, is a lack of interoceptive awareness; a person with the disorder is not in touch with the messages of inner experience, including hunger/satiation and emotions in general.

•For intimacy to be developed and maintained, emotional honesty and expression are an essential component of self-knowledge as well as knowledge of the essence of another.

•How will our lives be different when we encourage and embrace open expression of our full range of human emotion, including joy, grief, and anger?

•How will our lives be different when we are free to acknowledge our fears and our wounds without concern that we will be judged, scorned, or rejected?

•How will our lives be different when community really includes living with others in cooperative, supportive acceptance of selves and others?

INTIMACY ACTIVITIES—
SENSORY EDUCATION

These activities are designed to accentuate sensual awareness and to enhance your intimate relationships.

"...someone should be there to give instructions as to how to do total relaxation to remove tension, anger, and fear in body and mind."
—Thich Nhat Hanh

Sensory stimulation—
Self connection

Try this at least once per week.

- Stand with straight spine, hands folded in front of your breasts, elbows down.

- Close your eyes. Slowly fill your belly with air, raising your elbows as you do, like a pump bringing in oxygen. Squeeze the air out as you lower your elbows.

- Repeat three times.

- Pause and scan your body with your mind's eye, from toes to ankles, to calves, and on to the crown of your head. Notice any aches, tightness, or tingling. Wherever there is any, take in a breath of fresh oxygen and imagine sending it to that spot to massage it.

- Take three more deep breaths with "bellows elbows."

- Pause and repeat the body scan, this time imagining the tiny cells, tissues, organs, and systems as you visit each part of your body. With gratitude, think of how each serves you.

- Undressing slowly, take a bath or shower. Notice your skin's response to the removal of your clothing, to the air, to the water. Name to yourself each new sensation as it occurs.

- As you cleanse each part of your body gently, notice its response to the soap and the stimulation of your hands. Breathe in the fragrance of the water and the soap and your body. Listen to the splashes and the trickles and the gurgles of the moving water.

- When finished, rinse first in hot, then cold water. Taste the fresh cold water. Notice the aliveness of your pores.

- Luxuriously towel dry, massaging your skin with the stimulating fibres of the towel.

- With sesame oil or rich body lotion, moisturize every cell, spending slowed time nurturing yourself with your own touch.

- Choose clothing of fabrics that you want to be in touch with this day—soft, cuddly, comforting; firm, assertive, professional; slinky, slithery, erotic, etc.

- Pause 10 times during the day; tune in and name each emotion you are experiencing. Ask yourself how you are giving expression to that emotion. Practice.

Intimate connection to others—
Select one per week this month.

- If you have a partner, offer to share the sensory stimulation process with that person. Allow the sensual pleasure without sexual orgasm!

- As a gift for a friend, choose some delicious body lotion or oil with no added fragrance.

- Call or visit someone you know who is lacking friendship. Learn new things about them and their lives and share stories of your own life. Ask them to take a walk with you next week. You will be amazed!

- Invite a close friend or partner to dance with you in your own home with no one else around.

- Cook dinner with friends. Make a game of naming all the subtleties of each ingredient—its aromas, colors, textures, shapes, tastes. See how slowly you can eat.

- Play charades with scenarios depicting the various emotions involved in our lives—anger, happiness, sadness, guilt, surprise, fear.

Intimacy Project • Scarves

Braided Rapunzel scarves are easy to make, and are a good way to use scraps of yarn and fabric. These were created by Barb Mowery of Maryland, who "makes crafts in the woods."

Perhaps no fibre creation represents intimacy as aptly as scarves. Scarves, whether warm and protective or simply draped for adornment, touch our faces, caress our necks and breasts, and embrace us in close connection.

Think about a person with whom you want to create a closer connection. Spend time with that person learning as much as you can about their preferences and passions. The following are options for creating a scarf as a connector to another person.

The process

- If you already crochet, knit, or weave, create a scarf for that person based on your awareness of his or her preferences and passions. Select colors and textures that best represent these.

- If you are a novice, select a piece of fleece fabric in color and pattern that fits this person's temperament. Cut the fleece into the length and width of the scarf you wish to create. Hand or machine stitch fringe or tassels onto the ends of the scarf.

- If you sew and have access to old garments belonging to this person, cut swatches of these old garments, piece them together into strips as in quilting, then attach to a plain length of fabric cut to the size desired. Finish ends.

- If you enjoyed the finger-crocheting process in chapter three, create eight scarf-length chains in colors and textures befitting your chosen recipient. Join the eight chains by stitching with a darning needle using the same yarns.

- If you enjoy painting, buy a length of silk, hand finish the edges, and paint on the scarf, with fabric paints, images that capture the essence of this person.

- The Rapunzel scarf is the quintessential braiding of intimate cords. To create, simply braid three thick strands (at least 13 threads each) of yarn and/or strips of cloth, five yards in length. Add beads or other adornments if you choose, and tie off at the end. *Voilà!*

Present your scarf to someone as a gift of friendship.

CROCHET CONNECTIONS

It's not your mother's crochet; or is it? Think of the smart, sassy crocheted clothes and bags that are being created now. Everything from hats to free-form hangings bear evidence of the popularity of contemporary crochet. At the same time, old-fashioned objects such as dresser scarves and doilies are in high demand at antique shops and continue to be satisfying works of contemporary crocheters.

Do you know where the word crochet comes from? It is derived from the Middle French word *crèche*, which literally means hook. Sources vary in their opinions about the origin of crochet. Some think that ancient cords were made by finger crocheting (the familiar kids' craft of making a loop, using a finger to catch the yarn, and pulling it through, as in chapter 3). An early type of chained net—cheyne lace—dates from the mid to late 18th century.

Actually, crocheting probably began when someone discovered that a series of joined chains would hold together without a fabric backing. A chain stitch that could be worked without a background fabric was brought to Europe from Africa in the early 1800s. The work was known as "tambour in aria" because of the relationship of the embroidery hoop to the African tambour drum and the fact that the work could stand on its own.

Other researchers believe that "nuns' work," the embroidered embellishments for church vestments, altar cloths, etc., included crochet. However, though old religious articles have been well taken care of (there are stunning pieces that include bobbin and other laces as well as knitting that have been preserved), none include crochet. Some think that crochet was used to make lace-like fabric by ladies of leisure as well as the common folk during the Renaissance.

Others believe that wealthy needleworkers kept the poor people from doing embroidery because it would take them away from their household duties. Some even think that the scarcity of early crocheted pieces could be due to the fact that commoners were hiding their work because of this.

Crocheted doll's dress by my Aunt Caroline

Young women learned crocheting in the schools in the early days. They were taught to hold their hooks like a pencil because it was thought to look more feminine. Now, some teachers think that carpal tunnel problems are reduced if you hold the hook in the palm of your hand.

Early crocheting sounds more complicated in some ways. For a time, the back of the work was considered to be undesirable. Thus, the thread was always cut at the end of the row and tied again to the beginning. It sounds like a lot of work to me.

How do you relax? Is it windsurfing, listening to music, baking, etc.? Men as well as women find that crocheting can reduce stress (usually, if you aren't striving for perfection) as well as give them a sense of accomplishment. One devoted male crochet designer says the biggest drawback for him is being unable to try on the women's clothing he crochets. Like our friend, Tomas, many men are going where their creativity takes them.

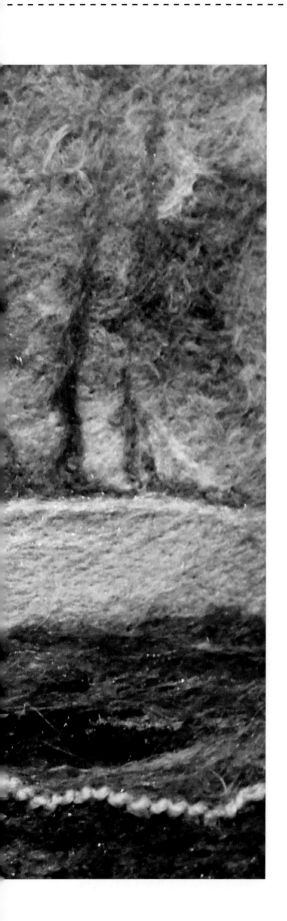

Chapter 6

COLORS OF CREATIVITY

Native African Prayer for Peace

Almighty God, the Great Thumb we cannot evade to tie any knot;
The Roaring Thunder that splits mighty trees;
the all-seeing Lord up on high who sees even the footprints
of an antelope on a rockmass here on Earth.
You are the one who does not hesitate to respond to our call.
You are the cornerstone of Peace.

Green Hills, *needle felting by Debra Poth of Washington*

COLORS OF CREATIVITY

"I always wanted to be somebody, but now I see I should have been more specific."
—Lily Tomlin

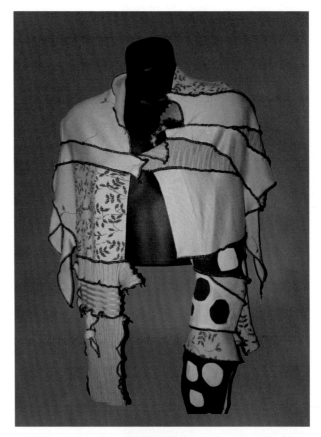

rtists can be easy to spot; they are often uniquely dressed, individuality seeping from all pores—in their words, demeanor, and approach to life. Fibre artists' garb is often wearable art. At one art exhibit and discussion, 14 fibre artists had created individual responses to artist Erika Mock's invitation to depict *Pulling the Wool Over Our Eyes: the Gifts and Metaphors of Fear.* It was obvious who the artists were; scarves draped artfully, dramatic hair, offbeat socks revealed them. Equally unique were the interpretations of the theme of fear, from political to personal, religious to mythical. What struck me as each spoke was the pervasiveness of fear in our world, and of how that fear inhibits our expression of our passion, of our creativity, of our full self.

Lunch and a visit to Erika's studio revealed again the flair that emanates from a true artist. Light from the enormous windows in her studio in an upper floor of an old police headquarters shed radiance on dazzling colors, textures, and an abundance of raw materials that allow the artist to "collapse the wave" of potentiality, creating new expressions. There were works of art on every wall and in every nook.

I was dazzled, not only by the visual stimulation, but by the courage and confidence Erika exuded. Courage is required not only to create, but to then let the world see and even buy one's work. In her workshops, Erika emphasizes play and nonjudgment as the ground bed for creativity; I believe these also instill trust in oneself and involvement in the process of bringing forth something that has not previously existed.

I ponder the role of fear in limiting creativity and resolve to break through some of my own. A perfect opportunity presents itself as a group of friends plans its next retreat at Iris's cabin.

Fibre artist Erika Mock of Wisconsin creates wearable art of colorful, asymmetrical design.

"Get out of the way! Let the fibres lead…they will form themselves into just the right combinations! All you need is to have plenty of colors and textures at your finger tips and start!" This was Iris attempting to lead our group in a session on creativity.

Iris exudes creativity! Her vibrant creations are called "Wearable Whimsy." Iris's attire smacks of it, from the juxtaposition of colors to the flair of design. She looks sassy in tight jeans with a hand-knit sweater tucked in, and she has the elegance of the opera in a flowing gown, draped with a classy woven cape.

Iris is a vocalist who taught at a local college until her retirement; she is a fan of opera and of tonal healing. She easily folds her body in two when practicing the yoga position of the "plow." Iris is approaching her late 70s!

Famous among us for her sweaters in as many colors as Joseph's coat and for her "full catastrophe" living, we look to Iris to ignite the creativity lying dormant in us. For differing reasons, the four others on a brief retreat to Iris's cabin allow only peaks and spurts of the vast reservoir within to shine forth. Deborah, a painter at heart who has flirted with allowing her artistry to appear, has a tendency to defer to the needs of those around her. Liza intellectualizes, exploring esoteric ideas, occasionally allowing her love of weaving to be expressed. Jamie's multitasking life keeps her scattered in many directions.

I am simply fearful of incompetence.

When I asked Iris about her freestyle fibre work, she became animated. "Working with fibres this way allows me to live in the moment, just watching a single strand of yarn become a 'piece' of something bigger as my eyes and fingers are drawn to the next color or texture. The piece seems to create itself through my fingers."

"Plus," Iris continued, "crocheting or knitting freeform shapes allows me to escape from the traditional rules. Taking risks is exhilarating. I enjoy the freedom of moving from one stitch or color to another without following any directions."

Iris, left, and myself in sweaters and hats hand knit by Iris. Her "Wearable Whimsy" shows her passion for creativity.

"I find it so exciting to watch each fragment grow as I imagine how these separate pieces might be combined to create a complete work of art. This reminds me of how the creation of something pleasing to myself connects me in a mystical—even magical—way to my mother and my grandmother who first introduced me to knitting and crocheting."

"I love hearing about the process," Jamie interjected. "How do you decide what each piece will become?"

"I make choices intuitively and spontaneously! I have enjoyed using 'free-form' ideas in knitting traditional garments that result in wearable art that is truly original. Interesting, I have discovered that my passion for creating with fibres and my passion and profession for music have similar elements—color, texture, rhythm, balance, form and unity. Is it any wonder that both of these 'passions' continue to provide never-ending satisfaction, excitement, and exhilaration in my life?"

"It is contagious, watching your excitement as you talk, Iris! I want to get started," exclaimed Deborah.

Iris has proclaimed this retreat "ignition" time, insisting that each of us is enormously creative—in the artistry of preparing a meal, the sweetness of flowers for a friend, an engaging presentation, a fresh way of looking at an idea, cleverness in helping a client with financial planning.

Yet, we envy the ability to also create artistically, and, especially, a hands-on process that results in something tangible. Like musicians who merge with the music, blotting out the external world as they allow sound to flow through them, fibre artists also express a spiritual relationship with the raw material of their art. Iris has agreed to provide us with a nudge toward connecting with that creative flow.

We woke to the smells not only of fresh coffee, but of baking apples flooded with cinnamon butter, which tantalized both our olfactory cells and our taste buds as well. Before indulging, however, we did yoga stretches followed by a massage of our vocal cords as Iris led us in chants. She then allowed a bite of the tasty morsels, but insisted on silent savoring as we did so…mindfulness meditation. The most sensuous breakfast any of us had ever experienced!

Next, we took a long hike through the woodland and along the shore of the rippling lake. The only vocalizations, besides scolding squirrels and cawing crows, were those of Iris, when she would occasionally focus our senses on a new fragrance, an extraordinary display of color on nature's canvas, or of a remarkable form, distinct texture of the bark on a tree, or of the graceful entwinement of its roots and branches. We each carried a basket in which to collect small offerings of nature—acorns, leaves, twigs, seed pods, and cedar flowerets.

Well-primed and loosened up, shifted into right-brain activity, Iris led us in a guided meditation back in the cabin. Sidestepping typical conscious thought, she led us instead through imaginary obstacles to a clearing into which we could invite all the creative potential of the universe.

While she left us to sit in this meditative mode, Iris laid out a plethora of yarns, wool, and ribbon.

Our only instruction was to create a representation of the obstacles to the full expression of our passion. We then set to work without discussion, each selecting raw materials and essential tools such as scissors and glue. An observer might have thought we were in conflict, because each worked completely disengaged from the others, absorbed in the creative process. When Iris finally interrupted, we were astonished that it was nearly noon. We had worked for two and one half hours.

We left our creations in our work area, used the bathroom, and did some stretches. Then Iris put on a CD by the Three Altos, gave us each a length of silk fabric, and led us in expressive movement! We finally burst into laughter and tumbled into a heap in the center of the floor, a colorful blob of undulating silk.

As together we chopped crisp vegetables and cold chicken for a nourishing lunch, we talked about our

blocks and inhibitions to our passions. Unanimous among us was the demand within to "do it right," with a fear of scorn or humiliation that ours would not be "good enough."

We set forth a covenant that there would be no evaluative words, praise or criticism, of our morning projects if we elected to share them with one another.

Our shoulders and faces relaxed when we were secure in the foundation of trust that judgment was contradictory to creativity. Encouragement for the process, the unfolding, the uniqueness of self, was our goal in sharing.

After a short, brisk walk to energize our cells, we settled in front of a crackling fire to share our individual creations.

Each was a powerful acknowledgment of passion stifled yet refusing to be squelched. Liza had created a human figure by twisting yarn around a small branch to form a soft body. The extending branches became arms and legs wrapped in felt strips, while unspun wool formed wild graying hair atop an acorn face. Bits of leaves, moss, and cedar needles became clothing. Overall, she had sprinkled and glued small pebbles which represented the "heaviness of rules" that Liza felt kept her from freely expressing her passions. Each of us could readily relate to the weight of rules, especially when they limit our zeal.

Jamie had started with a large rock. Onto it, she had fastened bits of yarn, cedar flowerets, and an array of colorful ribbon. It was so whimsical, it looked as though it could soar through the air…but, Jamie said, it was grounded by the rock representing her sense of poverty, of coming from "the wrong side of the tracks," which left her unable to "lift off."

For Deborah, the obstacle to passionate expression took the form of red yarns she had joined into a braided whip. To this she had stitched shapes in felt—each one representing a specific resentment she held

"The purpose of art is to lay bare the questions which have been hidden by the answers."
—James Baldwin

My mother kept us in style by creatively remaking our hand-me-down dresses. No one was the wiser.

toward some squelching experience in childhood, continuing into adulthood. Deborah's unresolved rage surged as she explained the times she had felt oppressed. Soon she was striking the braided creation on the back of the couch, decibels rising with each "whap." It seemed to provide cathartic release for her.

I had taken a curved cedar root that resembled a human figure bowed in humiliation. To it I had attached unspun wool formed into slumping wings, covering much of the body. Yellow kinked yarn, recovered from an unraveled sweater, became hair that draped like the wings, completely obscuring the figure's face. The coverings were the obstacles of shame that I knew prevented my own flight into passion.

We were spent. Sharing these creations which so deeply touched our "shadow"—that part of ourselves that we deny existence though it carries tremendous impact in our lives—was exhausting. Our denied dimensions become growth arenas when we bring them into the light where we can then transform them.

Iris suggested that we simply allow our creations to speak to us—on an unconscious level—throughout the evening and overnight. She encouraged us to spend some time with our image before going to sleep, keeping a dream journal ready at our bed side. She explained that creative transformations often take place at an unconscious level and may be expressed in dream work. We spent the evening playing with fibre techniques—simple knitting and crocheting stitches.

As we played, we discussed other dimensions of creativity.

Deborah expounded on the urge to express ourselves in some unique way throughout the life span, but especially in aging. At a recent gathering of friends, all retirees, each one gleefully told of his or her creative exploration: one was designing cards, another had taken up quilting, and yet another

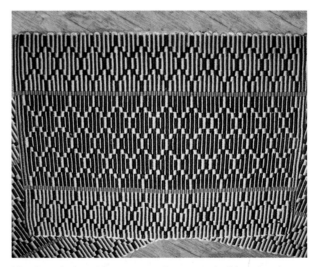

My sister-in-law Mary merged new and old technologies by using computer software to design these handwoven placemats.

"I would like...to see us take hold of ourselves, look at ourselves, and cease being afraid." —Eleanor Roosevelt

was carving wooden tree ornaments. Deborah was painting.

We marveled at the creativity of the ancients in recognizing the potential of fibres as the raw material of connection and how they developed the arts and techniques of fibre processes. Jamie pointed out that technology is also creative and that it has taken ingenuity to make the advances in medicine and communication and transportation that have occurred. I agreed, pointing out the use of computer design my sister-in-law Mary employs to weave her scarves, runners, and fabrics. This requires the merging of technology with the soul of the artist.

Liza offered recognition of the creative use of materials that people with limited resources make. It takes ingenuity to turn an old sweater into marionettes by unraveling the yarns, re-creating them into new forms. The indigenous women in Chiapas, Mexico, and in Thailand waste nothing, brightening their sometimes harsh surroundings with colors and designs. Deborah related how her mother ripped up old woolens for a woman whose income was produced by braiding these into sturdy, durable rag rugs.

My mother re-created in order to keep her five daughters and four sons in step with the styles of the day. My brother was a celebrity when he was elected class president wearing a multicolored shirt my mom had put together from pieces of worn-out shirts!

When I was chosen "Queen of Hearts" in ninth grade, I wore a pink tulle formal that Mom had created on the bodice of a basic white strapless gown that she had stripped down and re-created many times. We sisters had chosen different fabric to camouflage the basic gown so that no one would be the wiser, though our shapes and sizes varied by several gauges.

Iris read aloud a piece Katie had written for her textile guild, which synthesized the varying threads of our conversation in the essay on the following page.

Fibre artist Linda Bauer models her knitted and felted pieces at an arts festival in northern Minnesota.

Real creativity is not just beautiful works of repre-sentational art, though they are certainly one mani-festation of it. Primitive or not, one only has to look at the art work of children or the highly charged story art of homeless people to see and feel the intensity of creative expression. Creativity is like a gorilla in the room, exciting us and scaring us, too. Creativity is within us all; rich, super juicy, curled inside of us like a larva in a cocoon, full of curves and undula-tions, writhing, simmering like little string theory guys bopping around, waiting to burst forth like glorious butterflies.

As our creations of the morning demonstrate, often we struggle to release the butterfly from its cocoon. Early messages from significant people in our lives send us further into the folds of the cocoon. The chal-lenge is to create conditions that feel safe enough to invite our reticent butterflies to fly.

That is the process Iris has been guiding us through in this retreat. We'll see how many butter-flies—or, perhaps, moths—are flitting around the cabin in the morning. Off to our dreams we head, each spending a short time with our images before slipping into the comforters.

A celery-green luna moth lands on the screen door. She is beckoning. I follow her into a dark, damp woods, running for a long time, trying to keep up as she easily flits among the overhanging branches, emerges and soars across a large field. Then, we are climbing, climbing a mountain. I am breathing hard. I feel frightened as I must climb along a precipitous ledge, clutching at rocks with my hands. Just as I think I can climb no more, there is a step onto a meadow covered with lavender heather. In the distance is a very still glacial lake, mirroring fluffy clouds. Now I am alone. I cannot see the moth. I sit on the heather for awhile, so grateful for the beauty. Then I realize I must get back. The anxiety returns as I step back onto the unstable ledge. Suddenly, my foot slips and I am falling. Just as suddenly, I have the celery green wings of the luna and I am soaring.

I share this dream over coffee at first dawn. Everyone applies its symbolic message to the blocks depicted in yesterday's project, agreeing that it is time for each of us to develop our wings and to soar off the cliff into our own power and beauty.

The members of this group dare this morning to challenge the rules that bind us, the myopic focus that limits our seeing, and the shame that tells us we are less than. We encourage one another to experiment without judgment, explore avenues of expression that speak to us, and challenge the cords that restrict our "full catastrophe living." We agree to go out into the world passionately and creatively. Iris's ignition has lit a flame in each of us.

Inger Maaike of Norway created this luna shawl with the technique of nuno felting.

THREADS FOR THOUGHT

•Author and teacher of *The Artist's Way: A Spiritual Path to Higher Creativity,* Julia Cameron believes that our creativity is often blocked by injury. Her approach to unchaining our creativity includes practice.

•Sark, colorful and creative author, exclaims the importance of making mistakes, of laughing at perfection as we allow creative expression to emerge. From *Succulent, Wild Woman: Dancing with Your Wonder-Full Self.*

•Betty Edwards designates two ways of knowing and seeing based on the bilateral functions of the brain hemispheres. For creative art, we must make the shift to the right mode. From *Drawing on the Right Side of the Brain.*

•In his split-brain research, Roger W. Sperry, Ph.D., contributed much to understanding the functions of the brain hemispheres and their interaction. Research psychologist Robert Ornstein suggests the integrative aspect of the hemispheric functioning.

•"…right hemisphere…deep inner peace and loving compassion. I believe the more time we spend running our inner peace/compassion circuitry, then the more peace/compassion we will project into the world, and ultimately the more peace/compassion we will have on the planet." Jill Bolte Taylor in *My Stroke of Insight.*

•In *Creativity: Where the Divine and the Human Meet,* theologian and author Matthew Fox states that "Divine intimacy is experienced as creativity…which is accompanied by risk, surprise, and the courage needed for both."

•How will children develop more freely if, instead of evaluative grades and critical appraisal, each is given encouragement to explore and express ideas, thoughts, and visions?

•How will our lives be different when we as adults dare to be different, to express ourselves in unique and outrageous ways?

•How will our world be better when we encourage nonconformity in our schools, in our religious institutions, in our businesses, and in our communities?

•How will our lives be different when artists, athletes, dancers, "contestants" of all sorts are validated and encouraged for their efforts, originality, and growth rather than selected as "best," "winner," or "top?"

The *nuno* felting technique used by Inger Maaike to make the shawl, and mittens above, was created in the early 1990s by Polly Stirling of Australia. The process bonds loose fibre into sheer fabric, to create a light-weight felt.

ACTIVITIES • CREATIVE WRITING

Cloth-covered journal by Marci Glenn of Oregon

These activities are designed to nudge your creative muse in discovering relationships where none seem to exist!

Connecting within and without—
Try this several times this month.

- Spread a silky scarf, a nubby cloth, lots of colorful fabric swatches on a soft comforter in the center of a space where you can lie down, stretch out comfortably, and be uninterrupted.

- Place a notebook or journal and a couple of pens within easy reach.

- Think of some project or situation for which you would like to design a new expression. In the center of one page, write a phrase representing this situation.

- Formulate a statement of gratitude for finding exactly the clarity you seek, i.e., "I am grateful for finding this new approach to my business partnership."

- Spend five minutes with your eyes closed, humming or chanting softly, as you gradually make soft circles with all the joints in your body. Imagine fluid gently lubricating those joints until they feel supple and loose.

- Slowly come to a comfortable sitting position, on the floor, a pillow, or in a chair.

- Keeping your spine straight, but not rigid, imagine a golden cord passing through your spine, anchoring you deep, deep to the Earth's core with threads of the cord reaching in every direction, like roots of a tree.

- Imagine that cord reaching way into the cosmos, fanning out fibres to connect you with the "cosmic soup" of the universe.

- As you breathe in and out, imagine the tremendous energy of the Earth's core surging into your body, igniting every cell as it gathers in your abdomen.

- Imagine the "pure potentiality" of the universe pouring in from the heavens, igniting your intuitive inner knowing as it passes through the cord to merge with the Earth energy in your abdomen.

- Breathe into this image, with each sequence intensifying the sense of flow through you.

- Return to the situation for which you are seeking creative expression. Sit, breathing in and out, while silently repeating your statement of gratitude, for five minutes or longer.

- Pick up your writing materials and "cluster write" all the ideas and thoughts that come to you, simply scribbling them around the representative phrase you have written. Do not censor these and do not stop until the page is filled and you feel emptied. Continue to write on additional pages if ideas continue.

- Now, connect related ideas with lines. Does a new solution appear?

- If you are not yet clear, look at the writing intently, then leave it for several hours or overnight, allowing yourself to engage in totally unrelated activities.

- Do not be surprised if a solution pops out in the middle of the night or when you are not consciously thinking about the situation. If not, return to the practice and repeat the exercise.

- Capture your creative solution in writing, drawing, story, music, dance, or fibre.

CREATIVE PROJECT • FIGURES

*Since creativity involves the entire wave of potentiality,
nearly any project could be included. However, the making
of figures offers not only a huge
range of possibility, it also can
express emotion and meaning.*

*This project is an adaptation
of figures created by Erika Mock, in
collaboration with colleague Brenna
Busse, in a workshop addressing family work.*

You will need

- Scraps of fabric, ribbon, felt, yarns, buttons, treasures from nature

- Colorful unspun wool, many choices

- Floral wire, needles and threads

- Sturdy twigs, about 5"-6" long, branched or otherwise: choose those that exude their spirit to you.

The process

- Sit for a few moments in silence, noticing your thoughts, sensations, and feelings. What symbolism enters your experience? Color? Form? Texture? Allow an inner connection before beginning.

- Select a twig as the body, including face, of the character you have imagined.

- Onto this twig, wrap strands of unspun wool, roving, until you create the shape of the figure. Do this silently, noticing your response to the repeated motion of wrapping.

- Use ribbons, buttons, nature's treasures to develop the character you wish.

- Stitch and glue, wrap with thread or strands of wool until your creation feels complete.

- Give her a title or a name.

- Try writing a poem or story about her.

- Make a "home" for her.

- Make a whole family of characters, or depict the full range of human emotions. Or, use your imagination.

Stone Soup Woman

Figures in many forms are a favorite of fibre artists across the globe. Above, a garden sculpture by Kathy Fudge of Vancouver. At right, Merilyn Thomas of Australia used a similar technique to create *African Lady*. On opposite page sits *Jeanne*, a life-like fabric sculpture by Massachusetts-based artist Lisa Lichtenfels.

THE SOUND OF COLORFUL CREATIVITY

"Your right brain is your nonverbal and intuitive brain; it thinks in patterns, or pictures, composed of whole things, and does not comprehend reductions...."
—Richard Bergland, *The Fabric of Mind*

"Creative minds have always been known to survive any kind of bad training."
—Anna Freud

At Erika Mock's workshop, I needle felted my way to well-being.

• • •

Physicist Niels Bohr speaks of the field of "pure potentiality" in the "quantum soup" of the universe. All we need do is "collapse the wave" to create a specific new thing.

• • •

Psychoanalyst Carl Jung believed that human beings allow art to achieve its own purpose through them.

• • •

Our powerful negative beliefs, often developed in childhood, inhibit our freedom to express passionately.

Waiting for the results of a vaginal biopsy, I knew that I wanted to surround myself with two colors; orange and violet. I wore a deep orange sweater and wrapped myself in a scarf of lavenders, indigo, and orange to attend an Erika Mock workshop on Color and Story Explorations in Mixed Media Fiber. Color, like sound, impacts our psychological, emotional, spiritual, and, yes, physical world.

The science of color encompasses everything from electromagnetic wave length to choices of wall paint to personal empowerment, advertising, ceremonies, and healing. Fibre artists employ color science as well as intuitive response to create appealing combinations.

Tone, harmony, intensity, keys—sounds like music, doesn't it? Perhaps that is because sound and color occupy different frequencies on the electromagnetic spectrum. In fact, according to Dr. Kay Gardner, each musical tone translates into color eight octaves higher.

Music and color inform and are informed by our emotional states—singing the blues, playing golden strings, and humming pastel lullabies, for instance. Like music, colors symbolize emotional states as well: red with rage, blue with depression, yellow cowardice.

And, cultures have imbued colors with meaning used in ceremonial garb. In China, brides wear red while white is the color of purity in the western world. You can think of the meanings given to other colors—black, green, brown—and you can also think of music associated with these colors.

The synthesis of color, sound, and creative expression demonstrates the unity of all things and, according to ancient yoga science, is experienced by humans through our chakra system. A brief description of this is as much as the scope of this book allows. In the chakra system, there are seven whirling energy vortexes along our bodies. Each of the chakras has associated endocrine systems, life issues, tones, and

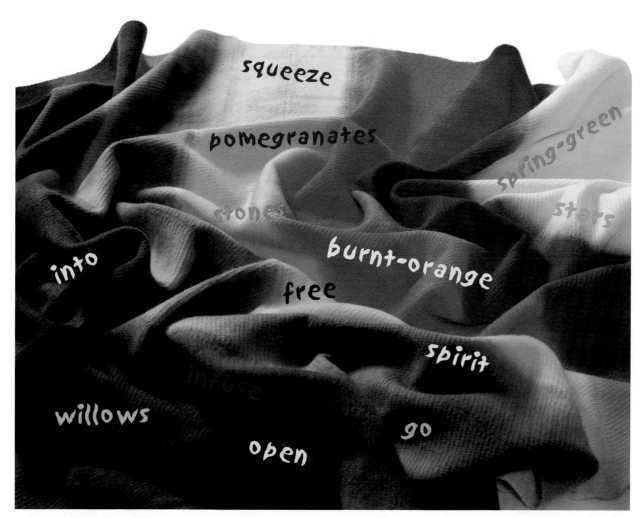

squeeze

pomegranates

spring-green

stones

stars

burnt-orange

into

free

spirit

infuse

willows

go

open

Chakra blanket by textile artist and tutor Steve Attwood-Wright, of Wales/Shropshire Marches, England

a specific color of refracted white light. The belief is that, when these are open and spinning freely, we experience health.

The seven chakras and related colors

Crown	Violet	Spiritual Opening
Third Eye	Indigo	Intuition
Throat	Blue	Expression
Heart	Green	Compassion
Solar Plexus	Yellow	Power
Abdomen	Orange	Sexuality
Root	Red	Groundedness

Healers such as Kay Gardner and Christine Page employ sound and color to treat ailments associated with the specific chakra area. Caroline Myss correlates each chakra to life issues and spiritual passages in her book, *Anatomy of the Spirit*. You can imagine, then, why I wrapped myself in orange, the abdominal chakra including the reproductive organs, and violet, the color of spiritual connection.

At the workshop, we created together a "word pool" from which each of us drew a handful. The words we chose became the inspiration for our fibre story project. The inspiring, symbolic words I drew from the bowl, "Squeeze spring-green pomegranates into burnt-orange stars," became a healing metaphor for me as I needle felted any potential cancer cells off into the universe.

The sound of my doctor's announcement the next week, "No malignancy this time," was a rainbow.

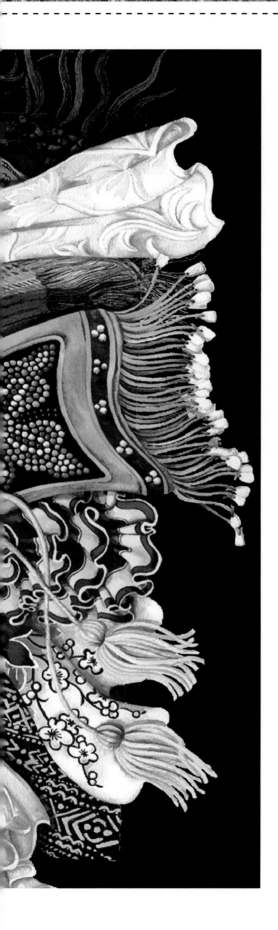

Chapter 7

WEAVING DIVERSITY

Jewish Prayer for Peace

Come let us go up to the mountain of the Lord,

That we may walk the paths of the Most High,

And we shall beat our swords into ploughshares,

and our spears into pruning hooks.

Nation shall not lift up sword against nation,

Neither shall they learn war any more.

And none shall be afraid, for

the mouth of the Lord of Hosts has spoken.

*Fabric of a Nation watercolor by Larisa Sembaliuk Cheladyn from
the Celebrating Women collection commissioned by the National Council of Women of Canada*

WEAVING DIVERSITY

"Weave, weave, weave us together,
Weave us together in unity and love."
—*Hymn by Rosemary Crow*

ey, Chickadee! I need more patches on my pants. Can you help me out?"

Madge's voice rises above the rustling of students moving to another class in the hall of the psych department. "Chickadee" became my nickname after a student camp experience.

Madge often wears a favorite pair of khakis as she teaches university students about marriages and families worldwide. Long ago, these favorite pants were threadbare at the knees and on the rear; a friend salvaged them with multitextured patches. Since the "Patch Lady" moved, I am her replacement.

"I'm staying at Uwe's for the next couple of weeks," I reply. "No sewing machine there, but if you want some hand-stitched patches, I'll give it a try."

"Hand-stitched are the best!" Madge responds. "Can I come over there?"

"I will ask if it's okay; but, you know, there is no kitchen, so I can't offer anything."

Uwe is a professor in the psych department; while he is lecturing in Germany I am teaching his classes. Staying in his home is an experience to remember.

Uwe and his Japanese wife, Masumi, inhabit small, side-by-side homes. Hers is serene, walls covered with her art: framed watercolor flowers, accented by complementary, three-dimensional paper creations. Simple furniture is low in traditional Japanese style.

Masumi's house holds the couple's kitchen where she prepares savory dishes that she shares with me when I arrive after a full day of teaching. I feel grateful, but uncomfortable to be in the role of traditional male, tended and served.

On one of those evenings, I have a chance for conversation with Masumi as I sip her comforting tea. She enlightens me regarding economic power in Japanese marriages.

"Women in Japan could not understand the feminist movement in the United States," she tells me.

Fibre arts and furnishings in the homes of Masumi and Uwe reflect her Japanese heritage and his international work and travel.

"Not until I came to live here did I see that it is about the purse strings."

Masumi continues, "In a typical Japanese marriage, the man turns his paycheck over to the woman. He only gets an allowance. Women run the household money. They will even buy the house. They save money by frugal spending and good management.

"When I came to the U.S. and saw that women were in the home with the husband giving an allowance, then I understood the movement. Japanese women never were so disempowered, so they did not need to rebel."

I ponder this concept. We discuss the impact of economic power on a personal and political level. The goal of cooperatives and of microlending organizations is to support people financially so that they may reclaim their power to provide for themselves.

As we talk, a framed piece of fabric catches my eye. "It is old, very old," explains Masumi. "It is silk, with floral designs accomplished using a special glue. My great-great-great-grandmother raised her own silk worms! Let me show you more!"

Masumi quickly returns holding a banner of a gentian flower surrounded by a circle. "It is our family crest, dyed with Indigo."

Opening a drawer, Masumi withdraws garments of intricately designed silk. She explains the significance of each. There is a wedding kimono, underwear, and a dress.

She sends me off to bed with a book explaining the origin of the family crest in Japan, with hundreds of pages of the symbolic designs. I am saturated.

The next day, Madge is delighted when I tell her that I have permission for her to come to Uwe's house.

"I'll bring a bottle of wine and some glasses!" she declares.

To appreciate the wonder of Uwe's home, I must explain his intercontinental connections. German-born, Uwe came to the United States to teach and to continue his work serving families with autistic children. He developed a project in Ecuador, setting up

Gifts from people around the world add to the rich mix of patterns, colors, and textures in Uwe's treasured collection.

Howard Bloom suggests that humans are "hard-wired for diversity" and that this diversity is a catalyst for creativity. He expresses the hope that understanding our drive toward diversity will aid in "progress toward (an) ancient dream —the dream of peace. We will always cling to common threads, yet stake out grounds for squabbling."
—The Global Brain

•••

Mensch is a Yiddish word for "a good person, someone to admire, someone of noble character."

"Fluid hardens to solid, solid rushes to fluid; there is no wholly masculine man, no purely feminine woman."
—Margaret Fuller, *Women in the 19th Century*

schools to work with special needs children and their families. Uwe and Masumi spend several weeks each year visiting her family in Japan.

Uwe has been officially adopted into a Native American clan. These are truly multicultural citizens. I am so honored to be welcomed into the home of these mensches.

Uwe's home is like a global fibre art museum. There is a faint scent of moth balls, probably to protect the vulnerable woolens from attack. Walls, floors, beds, pillows, and numbers of old steamer trunks are covered with hand-sewn, woven, beaded, stitched and needlepoint gifts from people on four continents. Down the middle of the living room hangs a long hemp hammock, woven in bold primary colors! Uwe has obviously touched many lives.

Madge arrives with two wine glasses wrapped in bits of patch fabrics. She pulls a bottle of pinot noir from the wrappings of her khaki pants, then looks around in wonder. "Oh, my gosh! I had no idea. Look at these artifacts."

Here's a hand-stitched tapestry depicting a verdant tree hosting a party of colorful birds. One can almost hear Latin music! Small stitches dedicate it to the professor in Spanish; it is easy to see the word "Ecuador" in the inscription.

A weaving in rough threads of tan, black, and white depicts three Native American figures.

On the wall are multicolored beads forming what appear to be Mayan symbols—birds with large observing eyes, facing one another. The entire piece is framed in threaded cowry shells.

More cowry shells accented by red beads decorate a straw basket on the table. A long string of beads rests within the basket. They tinkle as Madge lifts them.

Two clumsily woven dolls sit atop the couch back watching our every move. Coarse yarns shape the cylindrical bodies while black twine forms faces and hair, a single white thread creating primitive features. Beside them is a more sophisticated rounded stuffed animal, probably a llama. We conclude these are indigenous creations.

Woven woolen pillows with repeating geometric shapes in shades of blues and gray beckon from the seat of the couch. A large rug in subtle tones of mauve, blue, and gray covers the hardwood floor beneath the colorful hammock; the rug bears a label from the Amana colonies of Iowa.

The old wooden steamer trunks contain a history of their own which is hinted at through the slightly musty smell of the aged wood; each is covered with a piece of fibre art. On one rests a needlepoint of the entire alphabet, cursive capitals and block lower case letters, with a German signature. On another sits a densely woven woolen blanket labeled "Hudson Bay."

Hand woven runners in blues, reds, and gold with no labels cover long stretches of the floors. The bed is covered with a blanket I recognize from the desert Southwest Navajo weavers. Pillows in a variety of patterns, some Hmong, some Mayan, others unknown are scattered atop the blanket.

Madge sighs as we complete the tour. "It's like traveling vicariously across continents."

We realize we have not opened the wine nor examined the needy pants for possibilities; sadly, we discover we have no corkscrew nor have we needle and thread! We content ourselves to sit among the treasures talking and admiring the global friendships Uwe has fostered.

A phone call from Iris interrupts us; when I hang up, I tell Madge about the recent morning that Katie and I spent with Iris at her friend Tomas's urban condo. Tomas's home offers a contrasting experience, as awesome as this tour of Uwe's.

"How so?" Madge asks.

"Well, again, you would need to know the story to appreciate the wonder."

"Tell me, then!"

Enter Tomas's home and enter a world of fine arts. Symphonic sounds create the background while light tea fragrances waft among the notes. Dark, richly pol-

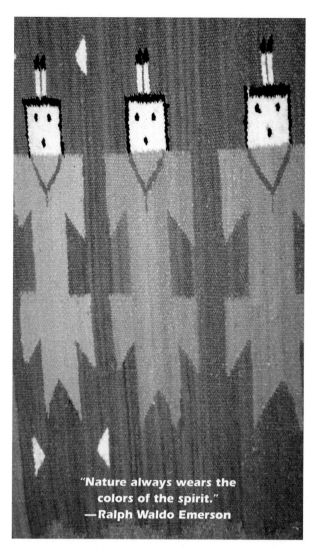

"Nature always wears the colors of the spirit."
—Ralph Waldo Emerson

Repeating colors and designs of the Earth are woven into Uwe's Navajo wall hanging.

ished antique furnishings are accented by collections of shiny sterling silver services. Cut-glass punch bowls inhabit every space not occupied by gilded lamps with fringed shades, porcelain lamps, antique clocks, and framed paintings.

Beyond the grand piano hangs a silk batik cloth in subtle shades of dusty blue and mauve, for which I lust. On every love seat, antique chair, and even on the floor are myriad cushions, pillows, and framed needlepoint pieces done by Tomas himself.

Tomas learned to love fibres early in life when his grandmother taught him to crochet. He discovered a penchant for needlepoint when he was about 10 years old, initiating a life-long relationship. He speaks passionately about the enjoyment he experiences in his work; in fact, he tells us that he was a bit anxious about our visit, so he took out a needlepoint project, geraniums in bold pink with spring-green leaves, to calm his anxiety while waiting.

Tomas describes his ultimate relaxation: summer vacation at the family cabin where he sits on a lawn chair, absorbed in his needlepoint.

Flowers are often a subject. Animals also. Not surprising are some very unique pieces related to his other love, music. This love accompanies him on trains, planes, and automobiles.

Teaching a niece the art of needlepoint is especially gratifying to Tomas. He is obviously touched by those who appreciate his work; he glows when he relates the delight of a teacher for whom he made a pot holder.

He describes technical aspects of his art also: thread weight, styles, patterns, and finishing techniques. At one time, Tomas was employed finishing the work of other needlepoint artists.

Tomas shares his home and his passion with the three of us. We discuss gender bias; he indicates, surprisingly, that he has encountered very little. His parents and brothers, as well as his adored grandmother, all encouraged his unique expression of self and that seemed to generalize to his peers and his community.

I finish, "Madge, it fills me with hope to witness this gentle man."

"Speaking of hope," Madge responds, "Laurie is performing next weekend at a cool event called *The Thread Project: One World, One Cloth*."

Shivers send goose bumps up my spine. Surely this is Rupert Sheldrake's morphic resonance at work. The universality of fibre connection is thrilling. I first offered *The Fabric Series* to a group of 12 women in 1996, its form evolving through the next decade into this book. Terry Helwig began her thread project in 2001, thousands of miles away.

Madge and I visit the website to learn more.

In anguish following the attack on the Twin Towers, Terry's vision was to create weavings of individual threads from people across the world, materializing global unity in the midst of diversity.

Tomas grew up with a passion for needlepoint.

Terry began collecting threads. She issued an invitation to every person on the planet to contribute bits of fibre from a baby's blanket, a dead soldier's t-shirt, a wedding gown, anything meaningful. The web of interconnectedness grew.

Eventually, Terry managed to gather threads representing significant personal relationships from people on every continent.

These intercultural threads were woven into cloths that are joined by donated handmade buttons into seven huge world cloths that are now on display in nations around the world. The project took five years. Its mission is to create "a global initiative celebrating diversity, encouraging tolerance, and promoting compassionate community."

We are awed by the stories on the website, stories of connections to the threads contributed from all over, stories of the connections that spread word of the project across the globe, stories of the 49 weavers in 14 countries who actually wove the panels, stories

Sophia's Mantle is one of seven cloths—14 by 7 feet each—woven for *The Thread Project: One World, One Cloth.*

of the spiritual response from people who view the cloths, each with a name symbolizing the powerful messages of unity intended.

Hope Materializing was woven in part by students in classrooms, and by a Guatemalan woman on a backstrap loom. This cloth is purple. Perhaps the regal, spiritual significance of the color strengthens the world's hope for peace and respectful community.

Threaded Harmony, Weaving Reconciliation, and *Cloth of Light (Lienzo Luminoso)* clearly speak messages of peace, while *Ariadne's Prayer, Dawn Looming,* and *Sophia's Mantle* invite explanation.

Ariadne of Greek mythology used a ball of thread to help Theseus find his way through a labyrinth. Her prayer is for humanity to find its way through the labyrinth of diversity into unity; indigo symbolizes intuitive knowing.

The rich orange of morning light in *Dawn Looming* signals a vision of a new day of harmony and true community.

The last cloth, *Sophia's Mantle,* represents "Lady Wisdom" who knows how to heal the world's tears by weaving them together. Turquoise unites the worlds of heaven (blue) and Earth (green).

"Wow!"

Madge and I are equally impressed by the unifying aspect of fibres and by Terry Helwig's persistence to accomplish this major undertaking.

As Madge takes her leave—glasses, wine, pants, and patches, untouched, tucked under her arm, she reminds me that we are meeting her partner, Laurie, and their friend, Aisha, at an exhibit of African textiles tomorrow. Aisha is planning her traditional African wedding.

In the morning, easy connection occurs as we browse the bold fabrics, stopping to explore the hand-loomed cotton strips of *Aso Oke* fabric sewn into head bands, shawls, and wrapped skirts.

Silk batik challenges us to resist touching. Lace shimmers in the light, accented by beads.

After 50 years, these little lambs finally came to life when I became a grandmother.

My favorite textiles are the striking *kente* patterns of Ghana with dark background colors in black, forest, or wine emphasizing gold and yellow symbols. Cultural significance is expressed in the patterns of the weaving, including wealth, nobility, family, and noble deeds. There is one, *Toku Kra Toma,* which means "soul cloth," created in honor of this queen mother's bravery.

Madge and her friends scan the exhibit for ideas for wedding fabrics while chatting excitedly with Iris about German opera. Bride and groom will have color-coordinated clothing and attendants will wear vibrant, shimmering patterns. Nothing borrowed, nothing white. I hope that I am invited.

Our multicultural party concludes the day at a concert by the Soweto Gospel Choir. The voices and the movements of this energetic group are as contagious as the multilayered traditional costumes, each in a different shade of luminescence. We imagine the wedding party as similarly vivacious. It is impossible not to move with the choir. By the end, the crowd is on its feet, clapping in rhythm, and begging for more. Filled, we finally part.

Too stimulated to sleep when I get home, I take out my new secret passion—embroidery! With the announcement of my daughter's pregnancy and my son's engagement, I retrieved pillow cases—started decades earlier—from my cedar chest. One set was given to me by my paternal grandmother, Marie, for my confirmation at age 15. She had crocheted a variegated trim on the bottom, and stamped the case with a scene for me to embroider, lambs jumping a fence. I had done a few stitches when I received them, made another foray when I was pregnant, and now have decided to complete them for Darci Marie's baby.

Another set was begun by my mother-in-law, Florence. I intend to finish these for my daughter Martiga's next birthday.

The third set is stamped with entwined rings, a gift from a high school friend for my wedding shower. Never begun, I decide to embroider this for my son's approaching wedding.

I am amazed at how easily I am able to create the delicate lambs, the colorful flowers, and the romantic rings from an array of embroidery floss. I am even able to re-create the crocheted trim my grandmother showed me a half century ago.

The reward is great satisfaction, but includes an additional side benefit; it engages my attention so much that I stay awake during those late evening hours when reading nods me off.

No nodding off after this stimulating day.

THREADS FOR THOUGHT

•Fibre work provides for human needs ranging from the very basic needs for food, clothing, and shelter, to the expansive needs for purpose, connection, and expression.

•Included in basic human needs, along with food, clothing, shelter, safety, and oxygen, is the need for novel stimulation. This means that we need new, different, contrasting experiences in order to function!

•Sameness bores us—addictions, TV, extreme sports, changing partners in trying to find novel stimulation. Human diversity provides novel stimulation.

Tarah Rowse created this portrait while in the Peace Corps in Belize.

•Healthy families are able to appreciate and encourage the uniqueness of each individual rather than requiring sameness.

•Exploring the vast array of fibre sources and textile design inspires awe.

•Learning about the amazing cultures across the globe also provides novel stimulation. Appreciating and celebrating this diversity is essential to healthy global relations.

•In *Spiral Dynamics,* Don Beck identifies essential foci of cultures over time and across the globe, as a model for understanding diversity.

•Not every nation with internal diversity should adopt Western-style democracy.

•Not every city should have a McDonald's.

•Not every person should wear jeans.

•Not every man should be a jock.

•Not every woman should become a mother.

•How will our lives be different when diversity is celebrated, embraced, and recognized as the stuff that contributes texture and color to the fabric of our lives?

•How will the world be different when uniqueness is tapped for the strength and beauty each culture contributes to the tapestry of the globe?

DIVERSE ACTIVITIES • MIX IT UP!

These activities are designed to integrate a variety of practices celebrating diversity!

QIYOLET

- *"Qi" represents qigong, an ancient Chinese practice of focusing the life force within and of subtle manipulations of our energies.*

- *"Yo" is short for yoga, a Hindu practice meaning union of mind, body, and spirit.*

- *"Let" is the last syllable of "ballet," but more accurately means expressive dance movements, beautifully demonstrated here by Chiaki Yasukawa of the Orlando Ballet.*

Connecting within—breathe and connect daily.

- Begin by careful posturing: plant feet parallel, big toes nearly touching. Straighten your spine, elongating your body with arms at sides. Tuck your buttocks slightly and allow a loosening at the knees.

- Focus on your breathing: inhale slowly and fully from the belly to the throat. Pause. Then, exhale by gradually compressing your navel toward your spine. Pause. Repeat 10 times.

- In fluid, graceful movements, raise your arms above your head. Spread them wide and spread fingers too. Imagine you are gathering energy from the universe.

- Bring your hands together above your head and slowly let the energy sink into your being as your hands pass in front of your forehead, your face, your throat, your heart, your navel, your abdomen.

- In full stretch, bend at the pelvic cradle until your outstretched arms reach the floor. Scoop handfuls of energy from the core of the Earth and imagine bringing them slowly up through your feet, your legs, and abdomen.

- Stretch your arms as far and wide at shoulder level as you can. Gather energy from all people, bringing it into your heart as you bring your arms together in front of you.

- Stretch your right leg as far to the side as you can while your left arm reaches as high and wide as you can in the opposite direction. Look up to the fingertips of your outstretched arm.

- Gracefully bring your arm and leg to center again. Cross arms in front of your heart, inhale, and rest your head on your folded arms for a second.

- Repeat this sequence several times, alternating stretches to opposite sides for the previous step.

- As the music moves, allow your body also to move in response to it—no judgment, nothing but flowing to the sound as you allow it to move your body. Imagine yourself a ballerina.

- When you have moved enough, stand again as a tall mountain. Breathe and notice the aliveness of every cell within.

Connecting outward—
Try this once per week this month.

- Switch your music now to some lively African or Cuban rhythms. Dance, allowing the music to move your feet, your entire body.

- Rest for a moment when you feel ready. Sit with straight spine, following your breath and again observing the life force within.

- Imagine the cells of someone toward whom you feel a bias. Can you imagine the same life force coursing through that person's body? Can you put a face on the person and look into her eyes while experiencing a sense of oneness? Can you listen to what it is that this person needs in order to feel worthy?

Expanding—
Choose one of these this month.

- Research the fair-trade practices involved in cotton production, particularly in Africa.

- Begin paying attention to the practices behind the fabrics and the garments you purchase.

- Visit www.organicconsumers.org/clothes for an article by Ronnie Cummins regarding sustainable practices in clothing production. The group's website contains more information on fair-trade cotton and the *Clothes for a Change* campaign.

- Investigate websites that list clothing manufacturers that pay living wages and provide humane working conditions to their employees—www.cleanclothesconnection.org is a starting point. Consider buying only garments created under just conditions.

Stand as a tall mountain—perhaps in a yoga pose. Breathe and notice the aliveness of every cell within.

At top: In Ghana, only men typically weave *kente*. It is believed that a woman doing so will be infertile.
Above left: Minnesota artist Mary MacDonald on portable loom. An Assamese woman working on a hand loom.

DIVERSITY PROJECT • WEAVING

"Some say our world is hanging by a thread. I say, a thread is all we need."
—Terry Helwig

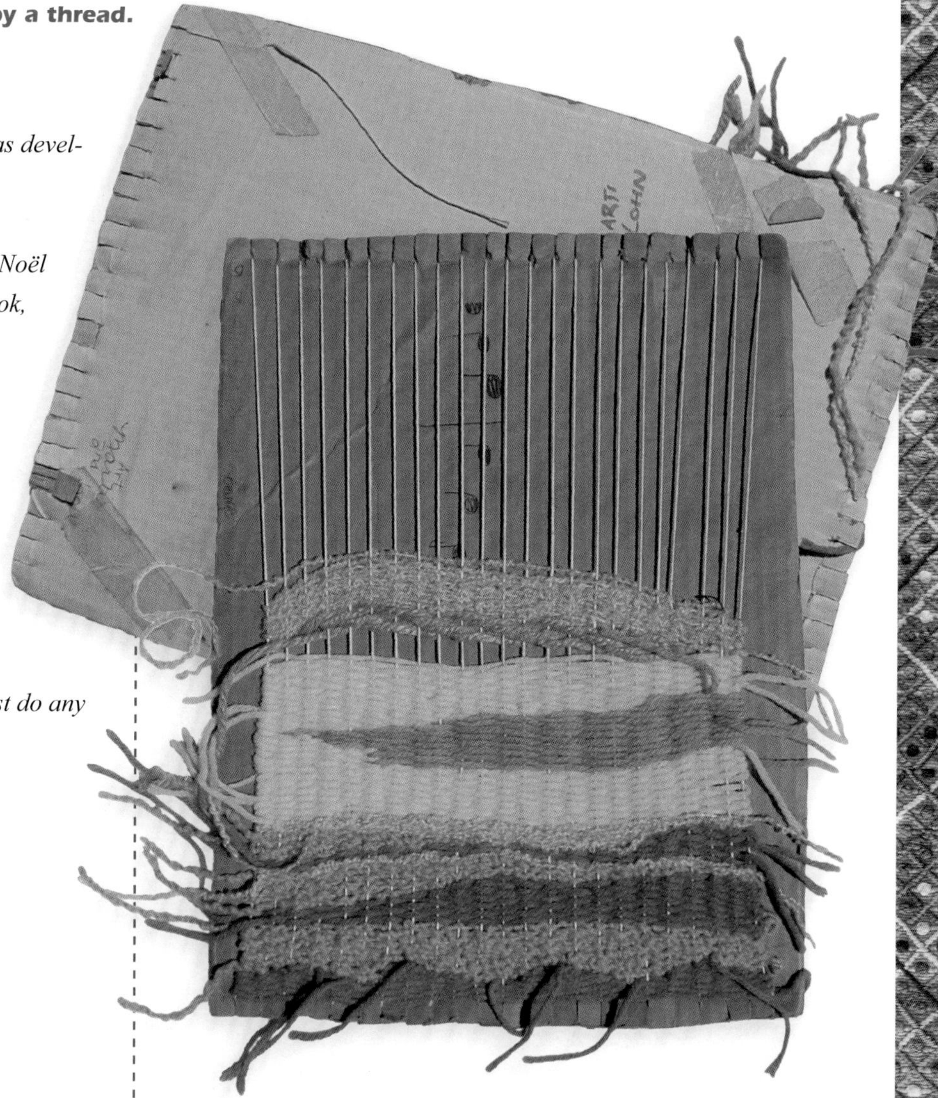

Weaving is universal—every culture has developed some method of weaving.

For this project, I have borrowed from Noël Bennett and Tiana Bighorse in their book, Navajo Weaving Way: The Path from Fleece to Rug.

"For Navajo weaving is meditative work that invites Woman into the energy center of the balanced universe. A place where everyday happenings merge with the mythical."
They quote a Navajo weaver:

"The root of it all is 'The Weaver's Song.' If you know that then you can just do any kind of weaving, all designs."

The Weaver's Song
With beauty before me, it is woven
With beauty behind me, it is woven
With beauty above me, it is woven
With beauty below me, it is woven
And in beauty, it is finished.

—From Halo of the Sun

So, with the song in your heart, and coming from your throat in audible sound, here is your weaving project.

You will need

- One 8"x10" piece of stiff cardboard, corrugated preferably.
- Neutral cording for the warp. (Warp threads are those running lengthwise on the loom.)
- Yarns in a variety of colors and weights.
- One dull-nosed needle or a smooth, flat piece of wood with an "eye" in it to serve as a shuttle.
- Two dowel rods, 1" in diameter, each 16" long.

[continued on next page]

DIVERSITY PROJECT • WEAVING

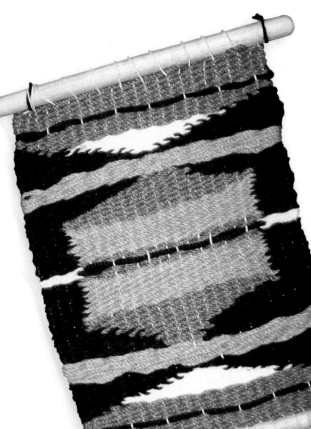

"*We all should know that diversity makes for a rich tapestry, and we must understand that all the threads of the tapestry are equal in value no matter what their color.*"
—Maya Angelou

A "Weaver's Pathway" is the contrasting thread that runs horizontally through the piece.

- Continue weaving, changing colors by tying yarn ends to one another, tucking the knot each time to the back side of your weaving.

- After each row, firmly push the woven threads together to make a tighter weave. (A comb or a fork is a useful tool to accomplish this.)

- Be creative in your colors and in design. Imagine symbolic connection to other cultures as you experiment.

- Savor the tactile sensation of the varying yarns, notice all of your senses in response to this process.

- Navajo weavers often include "The Weaver's Pathway," which is a small contrasting yarn woven from the outside edge into the weaving. It has a variety of meanings, including a "way out" of the never-ending process of weaving.

- Another practice included leaving a hole from which evil spirits could exit. According to one Navajo weaver, Shonto, "Without the *ch'e'etiin* (pathway) there can be no progress and no improvement." You decide if you want to include a pathway thread.

- When you are satisfied with your basic weaving, try adding knots, a fringe woven in, a shape, or a symbol.

- Finish your piece by tying all loose threads and feeding them through the loops.

- Remove the cardboard carefully and thread both ends onto the dowel rods; attach yarn at the ends of the rod from which to hang your creation.

- Hum or sing "The Weaver's Song" as you hang it.

[continued from previous page]

The process

- Using a box-cutting tool, or a sharp knife, cut slats in 1" intervals along the top and bottom of the cardboard.

- Wind the cording from one end to the other end, slipping between slats at the top and bottom, with warp threads only on the front, until all slats are filled with parallel threads.

- Secure tightly with a knot at each end of the warp thread.

- Begin weaving at the bottom of your "loom" by threading your first chosen color in and out of each warp thread. Be sure to leave a long tail which you will tie to the corner of the warp when finished.

- When you reach the end of each row, simply come back in the opposite direction, being sure to round over the outside warp thread. Inserting a ruler under alternate warp threads to hold them out makes it easier.

FLYING TIES • TYING FLIES

Diversity of sources and techniques is as fascinating as diversity of people and cultures. Paper-making transforms the fibres of trees and other plants into flat, fine writing and drawing surfaces. Ancient beading included shells, seeds, and sinewy thread to create adornment. Trout fishers have nearly perfected the art of imitating bugs through the clever use of both natural and synthetic materials with the aim of duping those trout into feeding on their creations.

"May I take some of this metallic thread in your sewing cabinet?" Bob asks as he assembles materials for a meeting on Wednesday night. "And, do you still have those beads left from your earring class? Can I take those also?"

This group of passionate flytiers exemplifies the interconnectedness of art, science, and sport. The "flies" they tie must "match the hatch" if they are to be successful in catching the fish.

Entomologists study the emergence of specific insects at specific times as this will be the only food the trout will eat at that time. Sometimes a hatch lasts mere hours. Anyone who fly fishes must know this as he or she selects the matching fly which has been tied for the occasion.

Materials and equipment assist the flytier in creating an authentic model of a given insect. Threads, feathers, animal hide, yarns, wire, and even plastic tubing are enlisted. Sophisticated vices and other tools allow the delicate manipulation of the various material attached to a hook until the shape, color, and appearance sufficiently match a bug to fool the fish into biting. As the hatch changes, the fly must also change, so a tier must have a wide array of flies.

For some flytiers the art of tying is more alluring than the actual fishing with the ties. Classes, expos, clubs, and groups of enthusiastic flytiers gather to share and demonstrate the latest equipment and materials as well as to demonstrate new techniques in the art. The passion for a well-tied fly is evident. The camaraderie shared by fellow enthusiasts is contagious. Intergenerational connection occurs as the art is passed on; Bob learned some early techniques from our grandnephew, Rolf, who had been taught by his grandfather Roger. Now he hopes to teach our grandchildren, Abbie, Riley, and Jake, as soon as they are old enough to manage the fine motor skills required.

For now, the connection is to his buddies. Bob raids my sewing cabinet one last time before heading eagerly out the door.

Bob's very appealing "Hex"

A transitional mayfly

Chapter 8

YARNS OF GENERATIVITY

Jainist Prayer for Peace

Peace and Universal Love is the essence of the Gospel
preached by all the Enlightened Ones.
The Lord has preached that equanimity is the Dharma.
Forgive do I creatures all, and let all creatures forgive me.
Unto all have I amity, and unto none enmity.
Know that violence is the root cause of all miseries in the world.
Violence, in fact, is the knot of bondage.
"Do not injure any living being."
This is the eternal, perennial, and unalterable way of spiritual life.
A weapon howsoever powerful it may be,
Can always be superseded by a superior one;
But no weapon can, however, be superior to nonviolence and love.

Women sewing in Bujumbura, Burundi

YARNS OF GENERATIVITY

"I slept and dreamt that life was joy;
I awoke and saw that life was service;
I acted and behold, service was joy."
—Rabindranath Tagore

Dancing for Joy brooches,
from I Love a Parade.

Hiking along the Gunflint Trail, rousing marching music from a nearby cabin elicits a hop in my step, a twirl of my willow walking stick. For a moment, I am transported—Joanne and I in the short-skirted, white, majorette outfits that Aunt Ann made for my sisters; tall, white hats with gold bands matching the cords across the jacket bodice; white boots; tassels swishing as we marched. Batons twirling, perspiration dripping, blisters forming…I hate parades!

Why, then, do I love the Twin Cities organization, I Love a Parade? Because of its subtitle: "Art created by your homeless neighbors." Sandra Haff is the generator of this organization that inspires action from the resources of both the homeless artists she employs and large corporate sponsors.

Katie and I visit her studio to glean more.

The old warehouse housing Sandra's studio has hard concrete steps with a cold, galvanized pipe railing. Creaky wooden floors lead into a narrow hallway lined with a variety of drably painted doors. Off to the left, an open archway houses a small restaurant that sends an aroma of freshly brewed coffee and something delicious in the oven.

We step inside to ask the location of I Love a Parade. The friendly hosts give us directions through this maze of architectural disaster ending downstairs in another hall of doors where a familiar poster signals our destination.

Drab building, bland paint, creaky planks effectively conceal a carnival of vivid, vibrant, expressive masks, puppets, and elegant dancers-become-brooches. All of the creations are of fibres—wild and staccato, subdued and sophisticated. Each has been created by an artist who is reclaiming her dignity and competence. Productive work, creative expression, validation of worth are all harnessed as each designs, produces, and sells her works, every piece carrying the signature of the artist.

Sandra greets us from behind a sewing machine. She is offering suggestions to an artist at work on a doll. From behind a bench pops a spirited four-year-old! Sandra introduces her as the daughter of one of the artists who is currently undergoing treatment; the child is living with Sandra during this time.

There are six women working at machines. Each greets us as Sandra makes introductions. Sandra's idea was born from her own struggles to find worth and work, discovering in the process that creative productivity accomplished both.

Already closely aligned with her homeless neighbors through a street ministry, the inspiration for I Love a Parade came as she watched the Holidazzle Parade one wintry evening. Sandra boldly requested the cast-off materials.

Parade organizers were delighted; thus began a gathering of excess fabric, thread, yarn, string and ribbon, paint, notions, feathers, and much more, not only from parades, but from theatres and drama groups.

Sandra's endeavor spread. Eventually, donations were coming in from large corporations and other sources who recognized that creative work, and an income, provided solid underpinnings for kicking addictions, escaping abusive relationships and a chronic sense of hopelessness.

Of course, not all of the artists employed in I Love a Parade accomplish what they need to do to become independent. Many do. Even a temporary period of generativity builds self-worth.

At an "ask event," the individual artists serve the invited guests at round tables covered with white linen. Flowers accent masks as centerpieces and a fibre-faced magnet marks the place of each guest. Classical music is accompanied by the clink of dishes and flatware in the kitchen. Delicious breads warm up conversations. Bellies smile as they fill with eggs boasting ham, veggies, and cheese.

Sandra stands to tell the history of I Love a Parade. Upon completion, she introduces one of her favorite artists, Carolyn.

Carolyn begins tentatively, speaking in barely audible tones. Soon every competing voice is silent. She tells her story of salvation through Sandra's encouragement and efforts. She speaks of daily drinking, having several children, her abusive lovers, and the threat of eviction. Carolyn had lost all sense of dignity, all hope for anything better for herself or her children. Sandra took her home, gave her money for the month's rent, enlisted nursery services, and required her to show up for work the next day, sober. Carolyn did. To her own amazement, on that very first day, Carolyn created a dancing brooch such as those above. She passes it around the tables proudly, having saved it as a reminder of her new beginning.

Next, Carolyn worked with another artist to create a mask for a display called *Found Faces.* Each woman got to know the other well enough to design a mask depicting not only what is visible to the outside viewer, but what lies within the essence of the person as well. One side of Carolyn's mask depicts an empty rum bottle, scars, and a toothless frown; the other side shows a warm heart, a devoted mother, and a beautiful smile. The masks are currently on exhibit, touring a number of sponsoring organizations.

When Carolyn sits down, there is an audible silence as people absorb the story of personal transformation just witnessed.

Then, questions fly. Sandra catches each one.

- Artwork is sold at art festivals, at the studio, and through the sponsors.
- Each artist is paid a regular salary for her efforts.
- Yes, some people continue to use and abuse chemicals; more are able to kick them.
- Contributions of money, goods, and time are readily accepted.

Sandra Haff personifies generativity—the capacity to initiate, produce, or procreate.

"People learn about themselves through the creative process. If you are able to produce something, you feel better about yourself and are then able to take care of other issues, like getting sober, for example," she says.

Sandra's commitment to this mission is matched only by her industriousness. Somewhat shy, Sandra overcomes that tendency in order to raise funds, encourage artists, sell artwork, and collect supplies. The organization has published a book with large photos of dolls created by the artists, along with each person's story. In the process of challenging herself, Sandra Haff is developing a legacy of "Found Faces."

Later, Katie and I are sizzling with enthusiasm over lunch with our 30-something daughters, generators like Sandra, with constant energy and initiative.

I've told Katie about the black woolen suit Darci made for me while she was still in high school, and the scarves, hats, and mittens Marti has knit.

Katie has described numerous projects that her daughter, Sarah, has created. One favorite is a baby blanket with appliquéd hearts of varying textures—smooth, shiny, and fuzzy. Sarah's six-year-old niece, Claire, still loves it.

The girls are intrigued by the story of I Love a Parade, and conversation spins off to other stories.

Sarah asks about her great-grandmother after noticing a photo at the house earlier. Katie describes the picture of her grandmother, seated with her three young daughters standing around her, one of them Marie, Katie's mother.

"All resplendent in wondrous white dresses that she had made. Beautifully embellished with tucks, ruffles and laces, they were a tribute to my grandma's skill and caring. She was a seamstress and a hatmaker, like many young women in Chicago in the early 1900s.

"Ali, my granddaughter," Katie explains to Darci and Marti, "loves that picture, too. She was amazed that my grandma could sew so wonderfully. You know, Ali wanted to sew at such a young age. Her mom, Margie, encourages her efforts just as my mother did for me. Even when I ran into problems, my mother had a knack for salvaging the project. I suspect that my mother's mother did that for her as well. I think how pleased my grandma, in her tiny apartment, sewing so industriously, would be if she knew that her work is so appreciated four generations later," Katie concludes.

Masks, upper left, one of the first projects. At right, Drugs, *by Sandy O.*

"Hearing about your grandmother reminds me of my great-aunt, Clara, who lived alone in her own home until the week before her 100th birthday," Darci says. Clara became an organizer in the care center after that. She died at 104. Her life nearly spanned three centuries —from 1896 to late 1999. On her own time, Clara knit sweaters and mittens, sewed doll clothes, and crocheted pillow covers. She was employed by a local clothing store, where she did fine sewing to alter garments.

Darci laughs as she remembers the story of this tiny, energetic old Norwegian. Even into her 90s, Clara walked 12 blocks to pick up alterations at the store, walked 12 blocks home, did the sewing, and returned them the following week.

On one of her deliveries, she fell flat on her face after tripping on the store's threshold. The clerks and customers were aghast as she had cut her lip and bloodied her nose. One shouted, "Call an ambulance!"

Clara righted herself and exclaimed indignantly, "I don't need an ambulance! Get me a towel, please, and see that that suit I just altered isn't messed up."

She was a tough old bird, kind of mischievous, lots of fun. She never knew idleness. I think Clara's work kept her alert and engaged in life. It undoubtedly gave her a sense of productivity and usefulness, so essential to vital aging.

She left a legacy in all that she did. The old country church to which she belonged still has several symbolic banners—hanging in the narthex—sewn by Clara's capable hand.

Marti reminds us about a tablecloth done at

Confusion, by Michell. She says, "Nothing matches; not even the eyes."

Moms and kids were thrilled to receive sweaters that Mary and others knit for the children of Chiapas.

"Peace is not the product of terror or fear.
Peace is not the silence of cemeteries.
Peace is not the result of violent repression.
Peace is the generous, tranquil contribution of all to the good of all.
Peace is dynamism. Peace is generosity.
It is right and duty."
—Oscar A. Romero, El Salvadoran archbishop

Cora gifted her pieces. I have one. It is a treasure to me and will be my daughter's one day.

We share other stories of generators and generosity. I tell them about the outfits my sisters Arlene and Beth made for me when they were teenagers, complete with braided accessories created in the warming house across the street. Arlene, retired from teaching, now makes fleece hats and mittens for kids in a school where children lack the basic essentials.

Pictures in my purse show the 30 small unique sweaters Mary knit for us to distribute to the indigenous people of Chiapas. Marti tells how a local doctor established a knitting basket in her waiting room, inviting patients to knit a few rows while they wait, with the intention of creating a shawl every few weeks for a resident of the care center.

Whether it be dance, art, or fibre skills, teaching is my friend Linda's natural gift. She has harnessed her passions by developing her business, Raven's Beak Design. Linda offers instruction on techniques as well as offers her myriad fibre creations for purchase.

All of these "generators" illustrate how much our sense of well-being includes contributing something, a knowing that our being here has made a difference, that we leave a legacy.

Whether it be mentoring homeless artists in creating fibre art from leftover material, sewing to clothe a family, sustaining the art of one's homeland, or doing alterations for others, we humans are enhanced by what we contribute. We matter.

Mothers and daughters, arm in arm, we five head out into the busy day. There is yet a lot of work to be done. I am going to try again to knit some slippers. They could warm someone's cold feet, even if my knitting is not perfect.

age 90 in Norwegian Hardanger by Clara's niece, Cora, in that same church. Marti launches into reminiscence of Cora's remarkable aging.

Moving back to her childhood home to care for her elderly mother, Cora was always in service of others.

She drove "the aunts" around town and on cross-country trips. She mothered her only niece whose father, Cora's brother, died young. She worked at church.

Cora's respite from constant service was holing up in her all-blue home to work on a piece of Hardanger, the fibre art of her ancestry. It is intricate work. Fibres are cut, pulled back, and wrapped in tiny squares. Hardanger requires complete focus. The resulting table cloths and runners are spectacular.

I think it is what kept Cora so active and vital into her mid-90s. Her penmanship remained absolutely precise, perhaps a result of the intricate finger exercise her fibre work offered.

THREADS FOR THOUGHT

•Work, productivity, contribution, paid or unpaid, enhances our sense of competence and self-worth.

•Uselessness at any stage of life creates despair and a sense of hopelessness.

•The third stage in Erik Erikson's model of human development, approximately from ages six to 12, is that of "Industry vs. Inferiority." Even children benefit by a sense of competence and contribution. Learning to accomplish tasks around the yard and house builds this sense of worth, as does fibre work.

•Adolescents who lack a sense of accomplishment experience a sense of despair: if their creative energy is channeled into productive work, they are less likely to act out through drugs, gangs, or violence.

•Erikson's middle adult stage is "Generativity vs. Stagnation." The task is to initiate, produce, and to leave a legacy. If we fail to do so, we experience a sense of uselessness.

•Elderly adults are several times more likely to experience depression and to attempt suicide than the general population. Loss of generativity contributes to this sense of hopelessness.

•In studying cross-cultural human development, Gardiner and Kosmitzki found that "feminine culture" work environments "promote gender equality, interpersonal contact, and group decision-making."

•Harnessing the creative energy of citizens of all socioeconomic levels, all ages, and all areas of interest contributes to global well-being.

•In times of recession or depression, loss of productivity contributes to loss of self-esteem, depression, and increased suicide rates.

•How will a new works projects administration contribute to our recovery?

•How will our lives be different when fair-trade practices ensure the work of each segment in the production of goods is valued and fairly compensated?

•How will our lives be different when a livable minimum wage is paid for anyone's work at any kind of job?

•How will our lives be different when handwork is valued for its aesthetic value and its connection to the person who produced it?

•How will our lives be different when "retirement" simply means a shift toward passing on knowledge, skills, and ideas through teaching and mentoring?

Clara's pillow, above

Cora's Hardanger, at right

ACTIVITIES • GENERATE GENEROUSLY!

"Let us remember that peace is available in every moment, in every breath, in every action."
—Thich Nhat Hanh

The following activities are designed to harness your altruistic energy in service of initiating and producing.

Connecting to self—
Try daily practice this month.

- Spine straight, feet planted, do five "figure-8" breaths: exhale fully, sending the breath from the center of your chest downward, into the Earth. Inhale, bringing fresh oxygen from the Earth behind you into the center of your back, between your shoulder blades.

- Exhale from the front, sending the breath upward into the atmosphere; inhale, bringing the air in from the back between shoulder blades.

- Repeat eight times, in a smooth, flowing pattern.

- Pause and feel your centeredness.

- Stretch out on your back on a mat or towel on the floor. Elongate your spine, feel the full length of your body.

- Roll to one side, lower arm stretched out perpendicular to your torso. Bring your knees into a right angle position, as though you are sitting on a chair.

- With the free arm, draw circles around the hand of the arm resting on the floor. Feel the shoulder massage as you do so.

- Slowly move the mobile arm (the top one) from the tips of the lower fingers, just touching the skin, across the arm, the chest, and then stretching it out as far as you can to the floor on the other side, opening your heart center.

- Pause and feel your heart stretching.

- Repeat on the other side.

- Now stand, feet shoulder width apart.

- Take 10 quick "sniffing" breaths. Exhale.

Recycling helps generate less waste. Scissors, fabric, and a little imagination can turn used containers into new gift boxes.

Expanding—connecting beyond self
Try these once each this month.

- Go to the resource list for this chapter. Select one worthy cause. Contact that organization and contribute—money, time, work, presence, ideas—whatever.

- Begin to define what it is you want to leave as your legacy. Take one step this day toward creating that legacy, another tomorrow, and the next day.

Many organizations worldwide provide opportunities for women, especially, to generate income by producing fibre arts, quality crafts, and other products. Employment in safe working conditions helps these women to overcome poverty, homelessness, and addictions.

Freeset's products help free women from India's sex trade. Signature tees bear names of women freed by their own generativity.

GENERATIVITY PROJECT • GIVING

Lap robes, soft blankets, shawls, and wall hangings serve as nurturing warmth and beauty for:
babies in crisis nurseries · residents of nursing homes
prisoners · women in shelters · AIDS respite care
homeless people in shelters · patients in hospitals
members of the armed services · a lonely neighbor
hospice patient.

This project is described for novice fibre workers; if, however, you are a fibre artist, I suggest you knit, crochet, weave, or sew your own version.

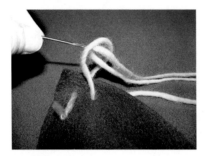  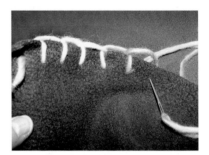

You will need

- 1-1½ yards of fleece fabric 54"-60" in width. Choose a size most appropriate for your intended project, though this measurement can serve well for any of the above. Select a plain or designed fabric, according to your wishes.

- One skein of yarn, either in a complementary color to the fabric, or in black.

- Large craft needle, with an eye large enough to thread the yarn through.

- An evening or two of quiet time in which to sit stitching, perhaps watching a movie or listening to favorite music.

The process

- Tie a knot at the end of a piece of the yarn, about 24" in length.

- Beginning at one corner of the piece of fabric, insert your needle threaded with yarn.

- Pull through to the other side, running the thread under loop. Tighten, then repeat at approximately ½" intervals around the entire perimeter of the fabric.

- Tie the end of the thread at the last stitch to the "tail" left on the first stitch. Trim.

- This may be as much as you want to do; as such, you have created a lap robe, shawl, or small blanket. However, you may wish to add a small pocket for a tissue or for notes of encouragement. If you want to create a piece of art for hanging, appliqué with felt or use embroidery stitches to add to your design.

- Make several and deliver your contribution yourself, or host a stitching party and collect these offerings from a group. You may increase the spiritual dimension of this contribution by passing each piece around, having each person touch it with healing wishes, as is the practice of a peace-shawl ministry.

- Teach this to others.

This fleece fabric with a northern theme required only a blanket stitch.

TOOL TIMES

Do you know what a bodkin is? Can you remember a darning egg? Anyone who has ever watched *Antiques Road Show* with the slightest bit of interest will find a look at historical sewing tools fascinating. Creative, beautiful, and utilitarian, they open a world of insight into our resourceful ancestors. Sharpened sticks, stone shards, and carved bones were probably the first tools used to sew skins into containers, clothing, and even shelter.

Now, a seamstress can create exotic works of art on wondrous machines with multiple capabilities. In between these two extremes there were many inventive and even beautiful tools. People seemed not to be content with just utility: hardworking clamps became objects of art as they were turned into beautiful birds; containers for scissors and needles were molded from silver into lovely little pendants called *chatelaines*; sewing boxes were carved, stained, and painted into special treasures.

Although some thought that women weren't capable of handling a machine that could replace hand sewing, many inventors began developing a machine that was called the "Queen of Inventions" by a popular women's fashion magazine in the 1860s. Although several were puzzling over the invention at the same time, Elias Howe is usually given credit for his design in 1846 of a machine that sewed horizontally. There is a story that Howe was struggling with how to make the needle do this. In a dream, Howe was being pursued by warriors whose spears had holes in the ends! This was his inspiration for the sewing machine needle. Ensuing legal battles with Isaac Singer resulted in Singer being credited with the invention also.

There were problems elsewhere, too. Workers in France burned down a sewing factory because they feared it would result in losing their jobs.

Many of us remember learning to sew on our mothers' treadle machines. I remember playing with the

For our eldest daughter, my husband updated my mother's treadle machine with a new Elna.

wheel at the base of the machine when I was very small. The cabinets of many old treadle machines were beautiful works of art. My husband restored my mother's cabinet, then inserted a new Elna as a gift for our eldest daughter. I still sew on my old straight-stitch Singer, our first purchase as a married couple in 1963. Used, it cost $100; we paid for it in 10 monthly installments!

We can all be thankful to our hardworking forebears and we now appreciate the luxury of having these wonderful machines at our fingertips. So...sew!

The brachial artery was found to have a large thrombus nearly seven

Beneath the lacertus was found a very large indentation in the median

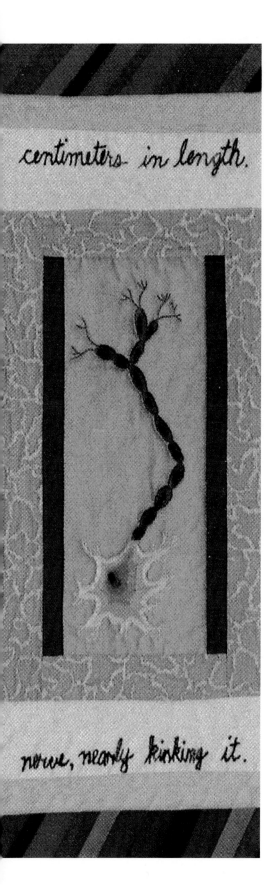

centimeters in length.

nerve, nearly kinking it.

Chapter 9

STITCHING THROUGH CRISES

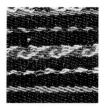

Bahai Prayer for Peace

Be generous in prosperity, and thankful in adversity.

Be fair in thy judgment, and guarded in thy speech.

Be a lamp unto those who walk in darkness, and a home to the stranger.

Be eyes to the blind, and a guiding light unto the feet of the erring.

Be a breath of life to the body of humankind,

A dew to the soil of the human heart,

And a fruit upon the tree of humility.

When her young son's arm was nearly severed in an accident,
Dana Fisher healed from the trauma, in part, by creating this quilt.

STITCHING THROUGH CRISES

Suzanne Marshall's quilt expresses dimensions of her journey through breast cancer.

The day was perfect, golden sunshine on my lush green hill after a night of rain. A cardinal sings its sweet song of welcome as my tires crunch on the gravel driveway, right to my open garage door. Yet, when Andy hands me the phone at five o'clock that perfect August Thursday, I know something has happened. Donna and I talk frequently, but we respect the priority of family and dinner hour. I take the phone gingerly and she says, even before I speak, "I almost for sure have cancer!"

My body shivers at the dreaded word. In spite of our awareness of advances in treatment and in cures, a diagnosis of cancer continues to feel like a death sentence. My mother died just seven weeks after her diagnosis of pancreatic cancer. This feels so similar. Donna had told me last week as we browsed the Uptown Art Fair in Minneapolis that she had to go back in for a second mammogram, but I had not felt much concern. My sisters had repeated mammograms and I have had repeat pap smears; each time our worry proved unnecessary.

I hear a slight moaning I realize is my own. She is animated, nervous energy, and rapid speech, as she describes the consultation she and her husband, Doug, have just had with a surgeon. There is a mass in her left breast that has suspicious arachnid projections curling from it. Surgery is scheduled for Monday. She has the daunting task of deciding by then whether to have a lumpectomy or a complete mastectomy if the tumor is malignant.

I am amazed by her ability to process this without tears, with little emotion other than the anxiety evident in her voice. I hear kitchen sounds and the sizzle of sautéing onions; someone is thinking about eating. I wonder how or why. We talk on about our fantasy of growing old together, *The Golden Girls*, and of our love for one another. Somehow we manage to say goodbye before hanging up the phone. A prophetic goodbye it was, for we were forever leaving the life with which we had become comfortable as intimate friends.

I wander numbly to my closet where the many garments she has sewn for me hang in a cacophony of color, so representative of the zest she is. I touch them one by one and hold them to my face, to my heart. I want to hold her and I want to be held in my fear. I feel cold.

Friday's conversation is much more upbeat. We both express optimism that the surgery will reveal only a benign mass. That will be the end of this crisis. I am able to direct some energy toward other aspects of my life, though my mind is still wondering, what if?

On Saturday I am amazed when the mail arrives with a package and a note from Donna. In the package is a purple tulle tutu. Accompanying it is a box of note cards on which are printed the words, "She lives to dance!" An enclosed note expresses her unending support for me as I struggle with current challenges in my life. She encourages me to live my secret passion—ballet. How like Donna to be thinking of me in this time of her own crisis, and how like her to express our friendship by sewing something symbolic. Dance. Zest. Life. Optimism. Selfless concern for those she loves. Oh, my beloved friend, mother, encourager. Please be well.

She calls early Sunday morning, telling me that she is at peace with her decision to have the mastectomy if the biopsy indicates that the mass is malignant. Again, I am amazed. In just two days she has made this major

"...most significant transitions...involve a time in hell. You go down before you go up. And most of these journeys must be taken alone. Having left behind a life that we have outgrown, we must continue the transition process to find our new life."
—**William Bridges, *Transitions***

decision and tells me she is at peace with it. I am not yet at peace with the idea that she is having surgery the next day.

In typical Donna fashion, she makes jokes about "carrying around those heavy boobs anyway" and "Who needs 'em?" We also talk very seriously about the impact of mastectomy and the treatment ahead if she has breast cancer. Always the psychologists who love to process to the nth degree, we discuss the impact on her sense of identity, of how best to support her as her best friend, and even touch on the topic of death. Monday looms heavy with possibility in every direction. Sleep eludes.

Bob and I arrive at the hospital waiting room following already scheduled appointments. I am touched by the supportive circle of loved ones who are there—her two sons, of course, but also close friends of both Donna and Doug who demonstrate the buoying of spirit friendship offers in the best and worst of times. Doug chokes as he hugs me and whispers, "It's malignant. They are doing the mastectomy now." I am only numb. My fingers caress the sleeves of the dress Donna made for me that I have elected to wear; I feel some comfort in touching what her nimble fingers have created.

Again, the strength of fibre in this dear friend shows up when she wakens from the surgery and laughs about the party going on in her room. The following days are filled with a staggering fragrance of flowers, an endless flow of friends, and light-hearted, avoidant conversation. We are all poised for the true prognosis, which will be delivered on Wednesday when the lymph node biopsies are reported.

Continuing to work, I call as infrequently as my

anxious heart can possibly allow. Late in the day on Wednesday, I call another friend who visited Donna at the hospital that day: 15 of the 17 lymph nodes taken contain cancer cells. We are told that, without treatment, Donna will likely live less than a year; with aggressive treatment, she buys a few years.

Again that moan that only slowly do I recognize as my own. I call her room and, for the first time in our 20-year friendship, Donna declines my call. I am alone in my grief, my fear, my aching, as she must also be.

I drive cautiously home, knowing that I am not safe to be on the road with tears blurring my vision and lightning bolts of emotion scorching the judgment in my brain. Once mercifully in my home, I sob my agony; I go to our guest room where Donna has spent many nights, has touched the pillows and quilt on this bed. I lie down beside the memory of her there. I clutch the quilted throw she stitched for me and sniff her scent. It cannot be that our days of delicious intimate talk, lusty laughter, and exploration of esoteric ideas are over. She is my friend, my sister, my mother who cares for me, tends me, and encourages me to become the best that I can be. How can I continue without this friend who calls me "Bestest" and fills my days with laughter and playfulness?

Fitful sleep, grief-filled puffy eyes, a prayer that it be but a bad dream begin the next day. I cancel clients and drive to the hospital, a long hour away. I tentatively knock on the closed door. Donna bids me in. We grasp one another in silent knowing, beyond words, just grateful for the moment of being. And we are both called to demonstrate the strength of our fibre as we face together this terrible illness.

Treatment. The plan is for initial chemotherapy for several months. Then, high-dose chemo in preparation for a stem-cell transplant. Donna, who loves clothing and frills and the fluff of life, demonstrates that she is more like her beloved linen than anyone would have known, toughened by use and agitation. She tells me one day, "I had to get cancer; I've never had any real hardships in life. How could I grow strong without a challenge?" She has never lost close family members; both parents and her only brother attend to her regularly. Doug, whom she married at 22, is not only a superb provider, but seems to take delight in supporting her shopping sprees and her joy in sewing more clothes than anyone could ever really need. Their two handsome sons call or visit almost daily. "A charmed life," she calls it. Now the charm is threatened. She calls forth her untested strength and we who love her can only follow her example.

I think of ways to support her. I decide to wear a "Donna outfit" every day and am able to wear something she has sewn for 14 days without repetition. It feels like validation of her right to life. I free my schedule on Wednesdays, take her to her treatments, sit with her, read to her, and we continue to talk through it all. We devour materials written about cancer survivors, about miracle cures, about the spirituality of the cancer experience.

We read about Edwin Schroedinger's cat experiment demonstrating that something may be so, but that until we know it, it does not affect us. From then on, our insider joke is about whether or not the cat is dead, referring, of course, to the insidious cancer cells invisible inside her body.

I design a symbolic stained-glass piece that my husband makes for Donna. Most meaningful to her, though, is something of fibre. So, I buy some soft, purple and teal fleece fabric in a lively abstract design, and awkwardly blanket stitch the perimeter. I create a contrasting heart-pocket, stitch it on, and fill it with handwritten notes of love and encouragement. Donna weeps when I give it to her and immediately wraps herself snuggly into it, pulling the edges around her chin.

It is clumsy next to the delicately stitched quilt her mom has already made for her, but I know that it means a lot. It unites us when I cannot be there.

I try to teach her yoga and meditation, but we both conclude that sewing is her meditation. When she is trimming a pattern, pushing fabric under the whirring needle of her machine, or stitching a hem by hand, Donna is totally absorbed. She is in a zone of peace, with no interfering thoughts of cancer or treatment or

My best friend, Donna, found solace in sewing during her long battle with breast cancer.

her dreaded needles. Between treatments, when she feels well enough, Donna sews.

She decides we should finish an outfit we had begun the day we had browsed the Uptown Art Fair; Donna insists that we could replicate a painted denim dress worn by one of the artists. We purchased denim and patterns and paint that day, but they were tucked away when her initial diagnosis set the world on edge.

When I protest, she declares that the focus of sewing allows her to live fully in the present moment, the exhilaration of creating the colorful design grounds her.

She likes feeling *chic* even as she loses her hair and swells up from the chemotherapy. Colorful scarves and sassy hats accent each outfit she wears during this time of baldness. She does bald like no one I've seen. One day I arrived at her house for a meeting of our consultation group to find Donna in a shiny, handmade, saffron-colored, one-piece jumpsuit, gold earrings, and bald head glistening in the glow of an overhead lamp, meditation music softly playing, with a gentle fragrance of baked cinnamon wafting in the air. I was sure she was a Buddha.

Doug designs, and has a jeweler create, a symbolic pendant while our group paints t-shirts with jewels on them in concert with the imagery Donna is using with her therapist in fighting the cancer cells. With so much love and support, surely Donna will prevail in this awful war.

Nearly a year is consumed by the treatment process. Following 10 days of intensive care in an isolation unit during her recovery from the transplant, Donna is finally home.

Radiation is the last phase of the treatment. She fares well. It is at the end of this that she finally hits the waves of grief she has so long held at bay. Days of grief, nights of tears, moments of terror briefly overwhelm the spirit of this strong woman. She tells me that she is grateful that I do not ask her to be cheerful or optimistic or hopeful as she goes through this dark passage. She isolates at times for whole days on her couch, snuggled in my fleece blanket or cuddled in her mother's quilt. And, in true Donna spirit, she gradu-

ally rises from the ashes to shine again in robust joy.

Her sewing machine hums happily as she sews a white brocade vest for her son's wedding. She looks radiant at the wedding with her very short, dark hair looking stylishly cut rather than barely emerging from the months of cell-killing chemicals. Months later, Donna absolutely crackles when she gets to sew maternity outfits for her daughter-in-law in anticipation of her first grandchild. When her other son also marries, Donna sews curtains for their new home and placemats for their tables. She delights as one and then another grandson fills to overflowing her heart's capacity for joy in living. And, she finds another fibre art that complements her love of sewing: beading. Now she spends as many hours focused on creating jewelry to accent outfits as she spends stitching the outfits themselves.

A psychologist, Donna has facilitated many groups. With the cancer journey so dear to her heart, she, along with a close friend, Linda, coordinates a weekly support group for women with recurrent cancers. All understand that once there is recurrence, the battle then becomes management rather than cure. Donna is a volunteer for the Reach to Recovery program that was so helpful to her following her mastectomy. And, she marvels as the years go by and, one after another, a group member succumbs while she remains cancer-free. We joke less frequently about Schroedinger's cat. Life returns to normalcy; we disagree politically and have a number of heated conflicts!

In August of the seventh year, I accompany Donna to her annual check-up; her oncologist tells her that he is convinced that there is now only a 10 percent likelihood of the cancer recurring. Donna looks anxious when she appears. Instead of rejoicing at this optimistic prognosis, Donna leaves the appointment telling me that it scares her, that the challenge of beating the earlier 90 percent chance of recurrence somehow seemed more encouraging.

By now I am on sabbatical with my husband in our cabin on the Gunflint Trail. In November, just before a trip with Doug and friends to Italy, Donna feels a lump in her neck. I do not travel the five hours to be with

Joetta Maue stitches her yearning for her husband in his absence.

her for the biopsy, which confirms her suspicion: the cancer has recurred.

Her voice message to me: "The cat is dead."

I am sorry to be so far away, though selfishly grateful for the distance that allows me a safe bubble of denial for awhile.

Now there are stretches of chemotherapy and rounds of radiation. Each time this resilient woman goes down, she seems only strengthened by the agitation. Perhaps it is no coincidence that her favorite fabric to wear and to sew is linen. She continues to declare that cancer has been a gift, has offered her rich spiritual depth. This strength of fibre will be tested yet again.

Zap…Zap…Jolt! Electrons firing in every cell of my being. Heart irregularities. Shocks…electrical shocks. All my cells are ignited…those infinitesimal vibrating strings of energy charged and firing.

"You have cancer." Eighteen months after Donna's recurrence, another phone call changes our lives, our relationship. It is my physician pronouncing the "c" word. An endometrial biopsy has indicated cancer in my uterus.

Hyperalertness. Unreality. My mind can't quite comprehend. I am the supporter, the rock on which she leans. Now, I must lean. She is gone again, on a trip. I have her cell number so I can reach her. I leave a message. Not able to be humorous with "the cat is dead," I leave a clinical diagnosis instead. "Endometrial carcinoma."

I can hear the quiver in my own voice. She must also, because she calls me back in only moments. And, Donna, too, acknowledges disbelief.

"No matter how many times I hear it, it never ceases to shock me," Donna says when we are able to talk. The quiver in her voice reveals her fear, even as she attempts complete rationality with me. Fear defeats rationality. We weep by phone.

Two weeks between diagnosis and surgery. Sleepless nights. My Bob enfolds me as I shudder my fear into his strength. I pull a soft blanket of fleece fabric around me like a cocoon as I struggle with the uncertainty; Donna's ready acceptance of her diagnosis eludes me. I do not feel finished with this life's journey. Among other pieces of unfinished business, I

The brachial artery was found to have a large thrombus nearly seven centimetres in length

eneath the lacertus was found a very large indentation in the median nerve, nearly kinking it.

Dan Fisher is the happy ending to his mother's quilted portrayal of the accident he had as a boy.

"If I could mend your heart...
I would weave together the ragged edges
Of your threadbare heart...."
—Mary I. Farr, *If I Could Mend Your Heart*,
a book Donna gave me near the end of her life.

keep thinking, "I did not write the book!"

Finally, finally, 10 days pass and I am inexplicably flooded with peace, unattached to the prognosis which will be revealed during a radical hysterectomy. I finally understand Donna's calm countenance. It is a "peace which passes all understanding." Following surgery, lab results arrive with an excellent prognosis. Anesthesia-blurred smiles on the faces of my husband and son tell me without need for words; I blissfully slip back into another realm.

Later, Donna acknowledges a brief moment of envy, then reclaims her own unique journey. Makes me think of linen. The strong fibres of her soul entwined with mine…beyond this life time. Donna sews soft yoga garments for my recovery and brings her beading to my bedside, making an array of earrings for every outfit I own! We snuggle under "blankies" we have made for each other in front of a "roarging" fire, soft music wafting, savoring, savoring this gift of the moment. And, we laugh about that damned cat.

For another year, Donna continues her struggle. It becomes clear that she will only have brief respites from treatment. A countenance of acceptance exudes. Donna worries about who will inherit the "blasted fur coat" that Doug has given her, and instructs Doug to let the women in her group go through her clothing to take anything they wish. She decides to make beaded watches for each of her closest friends and family members as a legacy.

As it becomes apparent that her life on this plane will end, we visit mortuaries and discuss her memorial service. Never losing her sense of humor, Donna, with her dark eyes twinkling, whispers in the gathering room of one mortuary, "Too small!" She knows there will be throngs of mourners. Wondering aloud if the country club to which she and Doug belong would host a funeral, she requests instead "one last party" there after the service.

When she asks me to read a poem I had written about her a year earlier, I tell her I doubt I will be able to speak. Donna assures me that I will, "for me." Of course I will.

As life wanes, her parents' minister visits her frequently; one day bringing Donna a soft, mauve prayer shawl, crocheted and prayed over by congregation members—people she has never met. She tells me, as she bravely faces death, "Now I will know the mysteries." And, as her spirit finally takes leave of her tired body, 10 years after her diagnosis, Donna is wrapped in that prayer shawl, snuggled in her mother's quilt and in my blanket, surrounded by those who love her most.

I am able to speak in tribute of my friend. I am wearing a smart woolen suit sewn by her able hand, with matching earrings and my beaded watch.

I wear them now in remembrance of her. The touch of them comforts me.

THREADS FOR THOUGHT

•The Greek root *krisis* means "to separate." One Webster definition of crisis: "The decisive moment; turning point."

•Crises can become opportunities for change and for healing.

•John Gardner, engineer of "The Great Society," under President Lyndon Johnson, says, "The nation today faces breathtaking opportunities disguised as insoluble problems."

Bead work of the Twin Towers
by Robin Atkins of Washington

•Grief is a process of recovery from loss, whether that be loss of a marriage, loss of an ideal, loss of a friend, or loss of a sense of security.

•Our culture affords little support for the grief process, even in the death of a loved one, certainly not for less dramatic losses.

•Healing is not synonymous with curing; one may die very much healed in spirit if life issues have been resolved.

•In *My Grandfather's Blessings*, author Rachel Naomi Remen, M.D., says: "The greatest blessing we offer others may be the belief we have in their struggle for freedom, the courage to support and accompany them as they determine for themselves the strength that will become their refuge...."

•Many people report that a terrible event in their life— illness, accident, death of a loved one, divorce, loss of employment, loss of limb—offered growth in directions they would never have considered—after the grieving of the loss was accomplished.

•Endocrinologist Hans Selye identified the neuroimmunological response of our beings to stress of all sorts, while cardiologist Herbert Benson identified the body's relaxation response, our ability to enlist the interaction of mind and body to counteract stress.

•How will our lives be different when we learn strategies for self-care to help us heal in mind, body, and spirit through all sorts of crises?

•How will our lives be different when we respond to critical events with support from others to express the full range of emotion?

ACTIVITIES • CRISES

"If we are restless or caught up in struggle, we cannot be at peace with ourselves. Therefore, we cannot be peaceful with others."
—Thich Nhat Hanh

These activities are designed to strengthen fibre and reframe challenges into opportunities.

Connecting within—
Gentle daily practice is good self-care.

- Stand with feet parallel, spine elongated, shoulders relaxed. Exhale deeply, with an audible sigh. Inhale, then exhale with a louder sigh. Continue five more times.

- Rub the palms of your hands together vigorously until they feel warm.

- Hold the warm palms in front of your eyes, not quite touching them, but feeling the warmth.

- With knuckles of your thumbs, firmly trace the line of your eyebrows three times.

- Massage your temples and your forehead.

- With middle fingers pressing firmly at the hinge of your jaw, open and close your jaw five times.

- With the tip of your little fingers, gently touch the bone below your eye at the corners, the center, and in the middle.

- Gently massage your cheeks upward.

- With thumb and forefinger, massage your entire external ear, tugging on the lobe gently.

- Pull strands of hair all over your head just enough to feel the waking up of the follicles.

- Pat your arms, your torso, and your thighs from top to bottom.

- With soothing music in the background, reflect for a moment on the challenges you are currently facing.

- Begin walking in a full circle around whatever space you are in; on each inhale, name a quality you want to strengthen. On each exhale, release some negative thought or aspect involved in this challenge. When you have circled the entire room, stand with feet shoulder-width apart and continue breathing in the positives, releasing that which you want to release.

- Wrap your arms across your heart, reaching as far onto your back as you can. Feel it as an encouraging hug.

- Learn the "Serenity Prayer."

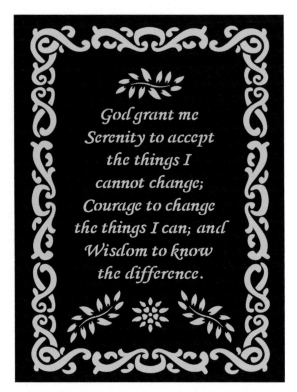

God grant me Serenity to accept the things I cannot change; Courage to change the things I can; and Wisdom to know the difference.

The "Serenity Prayer," as it is commonly known, was written by Reinhold Niebuhr, a theologian who did not name it. The piece above, by Cathy Fauss of New York, was created using a cut-paper technique.

Connecting to others—
Select one per week this month.

- Make a list of all the supportive resources available to you. Decide which to tap today, tomorrow, by the end of the week. Do each.

- Make a list of all the things in your life for which you are grateful.

- Think of someone you know who is dealing with crises of one sort or another. Reach out to that person through a visit, a phone call, a letter. Offer to be a listener.

- Join a project such as Linus, Afghans for Afghanistan, or a prayer-shawl ministry, and make something to comfort people in critical times. You will be comforted.

PROJECT • CRISES • STRING ART

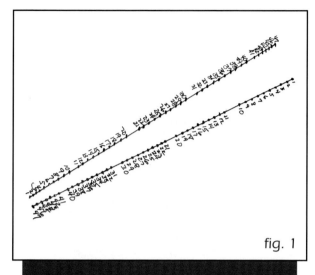

fig. 1

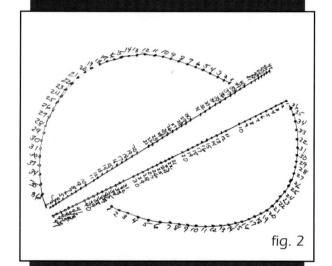

fig. 2

This project creates a beautiful symbol of turning our challenges into opportunities.

You will need

- A piece of tagboard, approximately 8"x11". Use any color that appeals.

- Heavy threads in various complementary colors, including black.

- Strong needles—not too large—to poke through the tagboard. Use one for each color, unless you prefer to rethread each time you change color.

The process

- On the back of the tagboard, draw two lines angled across the center. No need to be parallel, but they should not cross.

- At approximately ¼" intervals, place dots on each line. (You may have any number, but there should be the same number on each line and, in the next step, on each curved line. More numbers, and smaller spaces make for a finer finished product.)

- Number the dots on the first line; then, beginning at the opposite end of the second line, number an equal number of dots. (fig. 1)

- At the ends of each line, draw an arc or other curved shape fanning away from the center of the paper. Place dots along the curved lines at ⅛" intervals. (fig. 2, fig. 3)

- Number the dots in the opposite direction of the line, beginning with the dot away from the line. See close-up below. (fig. 4)

[continued on next page]

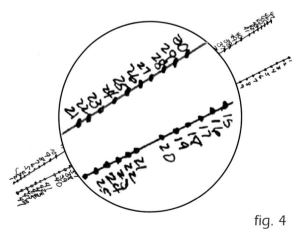

fig. 4

PROJECT • CRISES • STRING ART

[continued from previous page]

- Using a large needle or other sharp, pointed object, poke a small hole through each dot.

- Think of turning points in your life. Let each of the numbers on the two straight lines represent the challenges, losses, fears in each one.

- Thread your needle with black thread.

- Beginning with the two straight lines, working from the back, poke your first thread in at the "1" on the first line. Leaving a long tail so it won't pull through, pull the thread on the front to the "1" on the other line. Poke it through to the back. Stitch to the next number, poke through to the front and match that number, poking through to the back. Continue until all of your numbers on the two straight lines have been stitched with black thread. Already you have a beautiful creation on the front of your tag board! (fig. 5)

- Now, think of the resources, possibilities, and blessings involved in these challenges. Let the numbers on the curved lines represent these opportunities.

- Thread your needle(s) with colored threads.

- Working from the back, poke your needle through the "1" on the first curved line. On the front, pull the thread to the "1" on its connecting line. Poke through to the back, stitch to the "2" on the line, poke through to the front. Stretch the thread on the front across to the "2" on the curve, poke through to the back. Continue until all the numbers have been connected.

- Repeat on the second curve, again focusing on the possibilities and opportunities that could result in the challenges you have. (fig. 6)

- When all numbers have been connected, cut loose threads and tape the tails on the back.

- Glue your symbolic string art on a firm piece of contrasting tagboard; frame or display where you can be reminded of the hope it represents. (fig. 7)

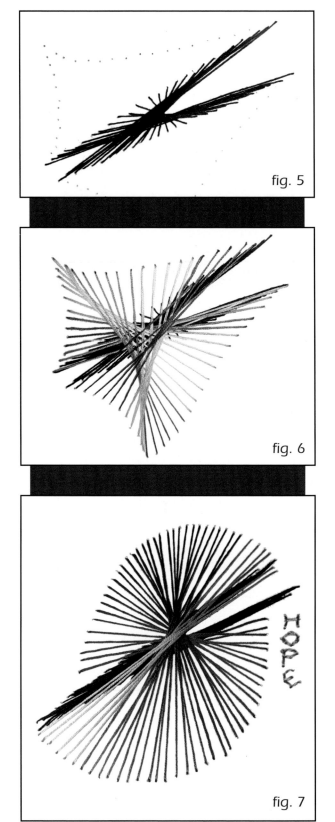

fig. 5

fig. 6

fig. 7

A PLACE FOR OUR STUFF

Titles often speak as loudly as whole texts. Virginia Woolf's *A Room of One's Own*, for instance, sparked the creation of spaces and places in which an individual could spend solitude within an ambiance of one's own design. Fibre work requires an appropriate space to house sufficient supplies and equipment, working surfaces, and a door to close so that a mess may be left intact. Emotional work requires an appropriate space to house our strongest feelings and to freely allow the expression of these without concern for outside judgment or discomfort.

We need a place for our stuff in our homes and in our beings. Developing such a space is often an act of assertion.

Artists have studios, woodworkers have shops, and hunters have shacks. Donna had a beautiful sewing room. Having an entire room is a privilege of the elite, but even a nook or cranny designated for one's "stuff" honors our passions and validates our needs.

These spaces require respect. Into these places steps no one without an invitation, and no other function should be served by these spaces. Having to pick up and put away so the table can be used for dinner or to tidy the place up stifles the creative process and interrupts the flow of ideas.

Living in a one-room cabin for 18 months with my husband taught me clearly the importance of a space for creative work. I tried to sew, he tried to tie flies and create stained-glass angels. The one table in the cabin served multiple functions: dinner table, game table, writing desk, project surface. Frustrating.

Fortunately, there was an old camper parked in the backyard; I cleaned it up, scrubbed mildew, picked flowers when there were some, and set up my machine. Productivity soared! We rotated use of this precious haven; when I finished a project, Bob would move in for a month or so with his. We both loved having privacy and the womb-like space for creative projects to incubate.

Likewise, we need a place for our emotional "stuff." Constantly having to clean up and put away our grief,

We need a place for our stuff — in our homes and in our beings.

our anger, or our depression stifles its flow. Instead of resolution, our process is stuffed. We need to honor our need for our deep emotions and insist that those around us honor them as well.

Our culture often requires that we "get over it" and return to the status quo, often more quickly than is required for deep emotional process. Authentic healing requires time and space. Creating such restores us to vital productivity.

A private place in my heart houses my Donna grief.

Chapter 10

RIPPING OUT, RESILIENCE

Buddhist Prayer for Peace

May all beings everywhere plagued with sufferings of body and mind
quickly be freed from their illnesses.
May those frightened cease to be afraid, and may those bound be free.
May the powerless find power, and
may people think of befriending one another.
May those who find themselves in trackless, fearful wildernesses—
the children, the aged, the unprotected—
be guarded by beneficial celestials, and
may they swiftly attain Buddahood.

This old "crazy quilt" has endured the rips and tears of life.

RIPPING OUT, RESILIENCE

"Hope is a waking dream."
—Aristotle

You notice her hands. Her fingers are contorted into stiff positions at angles painful to witness. Each knuckle has endured surgeries to retain mobility. You notice the twist in her spine shrinking her stature, making full elongation impossible. What you will take away with you, though, is the strength of her resolve and the tenacity of her spirit.

150 Reasons: Results Not Typical, from Melissa Devin's journal quilt on dieting (facing page)

That is what radiates through the weaving she began only after the diagnosis of her crippling disease, rheumatoid arthritis, when she had just entered her 50s.

Marjorie ventured out into the world when she headed from our small Minnesota hometown to nurses' training in Chicago. Years later, she moved to New Mexico, where she met and married Kenneth; there they raised their family. As their children were launched, Marjorie returned to graduate school to study clinical psychology.

Just as she was completing her studies, pain in her joints sent her to consult with a physician; the resultant diagnosis changed her plans and dreams as her life centered now around consultations, medications, adaptations, the grief for all that was lost…and pain, pervasive, unending pain.

Living in New Mexico surrounded by Navajo and Spanish American weavers influenced Marjorie, as she now turned to weaving for its therapeutic benefit to her aching joints and wounded heart. I believe that she wove for mobility in joints, for friendship with other weavers, for creative expression, for a sense of accomplishment, for meditation, and for the beauty of yarn, color, texture, and movement.

Marjorie still endures pain every day; she has not been cured of the nasty disease. Yet, she is the last to complain. She refuses to let her condition rob her of life experiences, so she adapts. Marjorie continued to ski, even moguls, for many years, still hikes whenever the terrain is flat enough to allow it, and goes along for the ride so that her family can take part in activities even when she cannot.

My big sister Marjorie is my inspiration for handling the ripping out, the "do-overs" of life. Her resilience astounds me.

A visit to Katie's college friend, Dianne, also gives witness to this elastic spirit.

Dianne is peering out the window of the front door as we pull into the short driveway fronting her worn house. She backs her wheelchair away to allow us to step into the entry, but pulls forward again with hugs and friendly laughter. Stuff is everywhere. Everything becomes potential for creating art, which Dianne prolifically does.

Her paintings cover many walls; one that captures my eye is a watercolor of a distinguished woman with silver hair. We learn that this is her mother. Several prizewinners hang in her bedroom. Flowers, fish, and butterflies appear to be favorite subjects.

Boxes are stacked everywhere. Some contain mailing envelopes with samples of hand-created cards stamped "Dianne's designs" on the back. She is submitting these to magazine contests. Her card designs have been featured in several already; she shares these with us when we sit at her table to talk.

Spring tulips stand out among the many eye-catchers in the crowded room. Dianne offers coffee and lunch;

This quilt was sewn by a former slave around 1850.

After losing five generations of quilts and fibre art to fire, a Louisiana family rebounded by creating new heirlooms. The collage, above, is by Katrina Parker.

she eats a prescribed menu as she aims to overcome obesity. A complication from hip surgery requires her to use a wheelchair. She is not feeling well after months of gallbladder attacks for which she will soon have surgery. Repeated hospitalizations for infections in her leg contribute to her immobility. Harsh coughs are interspersed with bites of food.

Dianne's health issues become mere background as we explore her many creative outlets. She extracts cards of fibre and paper and shares her accompanying poems.

Dianne describes techniques employing bleach, tidbits from nature, a scrap of this and a bit of that, often from something for which she sees a second use, items many might toss.

Quilts—she teaches quilting—are all created from recycled fabrics. They cover the beds of her children and grandchildren; we hear now about the death of her teenage daughter in a motorcycle crash.

Chemical addiction has visited this home repeatedly. It became a key factor in the breakup of her marriage; attending Al-Anon and living by its principles has aided her recovery from the divorce. Family members are active in AA.

Dianne was a music teacher but had no job at the time of the divorce.

"What," I ask, "allowed you to cope with the staggering reality you faced?" Dianne emphasizes that it was the principle of surrender, with absolute trust in "God's faithfulness to me" that has not only allowed her to survive, but to find joy and exhilaration in life. Her fibre creations exude joy. They are full of life.

Few of us will ever weave a perfect cloth from birth to death. There will be the dropped stitches, the broken threads, the cuts and tears of illness, accident, and loss; the challenge is to pick up the pieces and create anew. This is the inspiration of Marjorie and of Dianne. Resilience. Elasticity.

Quilters are experts at this. Living in a throw-away culture has not deterred the resourcefulness of these fibre artists. Piecing together bits of fabric, quilters create beauty, often from recycled material. Recognizing that old fabric, no longer serving its original pur-

In making a quilt about one of George Washington's slaves, Karen S. Musgrave battled her own dragons. Her blog quotes Stella Adler: "Life beats down and crushes the soul. Art reminds you that you have one."

pose, can be reclaimed and used again is environmentally responsible. Traditional hand-tying of quilts invites group cooperation, strengthening individual resilience.

Women of Indonesia, specifically those in poverty-stricken, tsunami-ravaged Banda Aceh, had formed a cottage industry of hand-sewn quilting projects before the big wave hit. Five died. Thirteen others lost their homes.

In the midst of terrible loss and desperate circumstances, a return to sewing helps reestablish stability in the lives of these women. Sharing their stories and their grief as they work cooperatively aids their healing. Scraps donated by other businesses allow them to sell the quilts to provide basic living expenses. The quilting cooperative also offers scholarships, medical assistance, and health education.

Emotionally supporting one another through recovery from the devastation inflicted by the tidal wave, these women are gradually returning to normal lives through their quilting.

When the AIDS epidemic began its terrible march through the human population, gay rights activist Cleve Jones stitched the first panel of the AIDS Memorial Quilt, in tribute to a friend lost in the epidemic. With his leadership, the quilt became the largest community fibre project in the world, panels from around the globe memorializing victims of this disease. Displays of the more than 44,000 individual panels have generated millions of dollars for fighting AIDS.

The Quilters of Gee's Bend individually create symbols of their life story for quilt surfaces, then work together to join the pieces. This unique group of African American women exemplifies the resilience and

After visiting Sichuan, China, Hong Kong-based artist/photographer Hazel Chiu dedicated a quilt of blessings to children who died in the earthquake there. Quilting helped soothe her after her grandmother's passing.

strength of women, intergenerationally, to combine art, story, and utility as they meet the challenges of life. The quilts were originally intended for personal use, but were recognized as fine art and now command six-figure price tags. These spectacular hand-tied quilts have been featured on U.S. postage stamps and are on display at prestigious art museums.

In an old issue of *Ms. Magazine* (March/April, 1992), author Mary Kay Blakely relates a story titled "Quilting New Networks." It was her response to the fourth annual Ms. Foundation Institute on Women and Economic Development, "a forum designed to achieve economic self-determination for low-income women."

Her impassioned article discusses this gathering of women seeking to establish "a compassion-driven economics, where money is carefully distributed in small increments wherever it is most needed." Blakely discusses a number of efforts at this, the most famous

being a microcredit lending program, administered by the Grameen Bank in Bangladesh.

Muhammad Yunus and the Grameen Bank were awarded the Nobel Prize for Peace in 2006 for this successful endeavor to make money available in small amounts to "...the self-employed poor, allowing market vendors, backyard mechanics, seamstresses, shoemakers, carpenters, and others to free themselves from loan sharks..."

Social entrepreneurship is an umbrella term for individuals and organizations addressing social problems through economics. Nonprofit as well as for-profit endeavors aim to assist the marginalized through novel means. Women's cooperatives often assist fibre workers in producing and selling their work to provide family income. These now exist across the globe.

Blakely sums up the culmination of the economic forum with this moving account (on following page) in response to the Pat Ferrero film, *Hearts and Hands*:

> **"Something within us can transform suffering into wisdom"**
> —Rachel Naomi Remen

...the history of women's sewing, a major thread in the story of female enterprise. In previous generations the quilt was like a market share traded for vegetables or grains or, in the case of one black seamstress in the South, for freedom. The beauty of the quilt was that when materials were in short supply during wars and famines, it could be made from scraps.

Women cut up their wedding dresses during hard times and sewed nonstop through revolutionary wars, Midwestern droughts, months in covered wagons. Their quilts were sold to raise money for the temperance movement, hung in yards with coded messages for underground railroad conductors, raffled in fundraisers for frontier hospitals.

A period of "crazy quilts" emerged during the 1800s, when women were without patterns and had to invent. With a needle and thread and a few scraps of fabric, enterprising women supported large families, saved farms, and kept a whole country warm.

Blakely ends with a rallying cry to join the "Crazy Quilt Army!"

And that cry evokes an image of a quilt hanging over the back of my husband's favorite rocking chair, the one in which he snuggles for naps in warm beams of sunlight on crisp winter days. The quilt consists of earth-toned flannel squares, large and small, with appliquéd North Woods birds. The squares are joined with frayed edges out, creating a textured, fringed look; the frayed edges remind me of the tears in the lives of the women who put it together. It was given to me years ago by a friend who participated in a therapy group as she struggled with schizophrenia.

Bonnie, a physician's assistant, was a beauty queen, an accomplished seamstress, and a cook whose gourmet meals were to be envied. Bonnie married, had two children, then began to unravel.

Early in her 30s, she was diagnosed with schizophrenia. Her marriage ended, she could not continue to work, lost custody of her children, and had no place to live.

Reluctantly, Bonnie finally accepted help from social services where she soon connected with Jane, a dedicated, creative social worker. Gradually engendering Bonnie's trust, Jane helped her obtain disability benefits, a sheltered apartment, and a renewed sense of competence and dignity.

Though Bonnie resisted at first, Jane convinced her to see a psychiatrist for medication to help manage her illness. And, Jane coaxed Bonnie to participate in a group she conducts for clients with persistent mental disabilities.

This "humility block" by Nicole Shyne Reed shows the quilter's intentional flaw.

One day, she finally showed up. Standing against the wall, near the door the entire first session, Bonnie checked out the other members of the group and Jane as the leader. They met the test. She decided they could be trusted. The next week, Bonnie sat among them as they devoured pizza and simply talked. Within a month, Bonnie shared her sewing and knitting proficiency by bringing in dolls and a multitude of doll clothes she had made for her community's orphan project. Creative Jane decided to harness those skills in therapeutic service for the group.

Quilting offered exactly what Jane knew would benefit the group. Creativity, competence, contribution, and social connection in the process. She tapped Bonnie's natural leadership, as well as her sewing skills and generosity, in asking her to lead the process.

Bonnie stepped up to the task. She soon took over. The group members each designed and stitched squares around an agreed-upon theme, then worked together to join the squares and finish the quilt. Tenta-

Former *Project Runway* contestant Jack Mackenroth shows his *Living Positive by Design* quilt. It was made by volunteers as part of his HIV education campaign. Jack hopes that the quilt will join the Names (AIDS) Quilt Project.

appropriate recipients of these quilts. Soon the residents of the local nursing home were receiving lap quilts in honor of their birthdays, a women's shelter covered its beds with the quilts, and each group member took one home to share with someone they cared about.

More than the quilts, though, these women stitched themselves back to a new wholeness. Bonnie, still on medication, is an active community member and has reestablished regular visits with her children. She sews impeccable outfits for herself, reigniting the beauty that had vanished into her illness for many years. In fact, she has a boyfriend who accompanies her on her missions of quilt delivery!

Others in the group have demonstrated less dramatic, nonetheless substantial, changes in their health and well-being.

Like the characters in *The Wizard of Oz,* we discover that we have within us exactly what it is we really need and long for, once we stop seeking a magical fix from an outer source.

Resilience—the ability to bounce back. Rebuilding after devastation.

Re-, meaning "to do again," is an important prefix if we are to survive the rips and tears of life. Important for the reclamation of our souls…the valuing of hand work. Redo, recycle, reclaim, reuse, restore. Important if our planet is to survive the abuse we have inflicted.

After a phone conversation with Bonnie, I dig in my "fix-it" drawer to find an old quilt that belonged to my mother-in-law, Florence. It is in need of much repair. I have saved bits of cotton fabric for years, thinking of restoring it. I remember Florence's resilience after losing her husband at age 42, with four young children to raise. She recovered, worked as a college librarian, traveled the world, hooked self-designed rugs, taught my daughter the art, and remained always open to new horizons.

Elasticity. I will ask Bob to help me work on this quilt through the coming winter months.

tive at first, before long, members were making suggestions to one another, helping when someone had a difficult corner to stitch, and envisioning new designs.

By the time the first project was complete, the group members were making jokes, laughing about life's unexpected rips, and offering bits of advice for mending these. Much more than a quilt was being redone. And, the proud satisfaction shining from their faces as they held up the first finished piece of art warmed the room. When Jane suggested they make more quilts, every group member enthusiastically cheered!

Bonnie's enormous altruism required that she research

THREADS FOR THOUGHT

•Resilience is the ability to adapt to difficulty in life.

•Most people do bounce back from challenges after a period of adjustment.

•Supportive connection to others is a significant factor in recovering from grief and other trauma.

•A sense of competence is also important, as is the ability to accept change.

In this *Leaving Us* quilt, Cheryl Lynch documents her father's Alzheimer's.

•Being able to talk about, repeatedly, our losses and our fears helps us come to terms with them.

•How will our lives be different when we feel no need to apologize for our tears and depression in time of loss, even when these occur months and years later?

•How will our lives be different when we recognize that change and loss require process time during which we need ongoing support, encouragement, and understanding?

•Mental and emotional disorders impact lives as powerfully as physical disorders, but often are accompanied by social stigma.

•Resilience includes experiencing the strong emotions of loss while managing them and taking realistic action.

•The Chinese compare life's transitions to "crossing the great river," in which one leaves the security of one side, steps into muddy, turbulent waters with no view of the other bank, then swims determinedly to get across.

•In a time of grief or trauma, there is a period of disorientation, sometimes lengthy, during which it is often important to rely on others for major decisions.

•How will our lives be different when bereavement leave includes the grief of divorce, natural disaster, emotional and physical illness, and is thus honored with time off, massages, gifted meals, and greeting cards?

•How will our lives be different when community supports one another even when there is no major catastrophic event?

Cheerful little dresses are brightening up young lives.

Connecting inward—Gently practice this several times per week this month.

- Play soft, soothing music, preferably lullabies.

- Spread a soft quilt or two in the center of the room.*

- Lie comfortably on the quilt, gently rolling and rocking as you are moved to do so.

- Draw circles in the air with all of your joints to give them each a gentle lubrication.

- Wherever you have pain, stiffness, aches, draw in a deep breath and imagine sending the healing oxygen to that very spot. Repeat several times. Notice.

- Extend each appendage to its full length, one by one.

- Rest on your belly, focusing on the places where your body meets the support of the Earth.

- Caress the quilt, connecting to those who created it.

- Come slowly to a comfortable sitting position. Focus on regular, rhythmic breathing; sit for a few moments.

- Think of the tears and rips in your life. Allow yourself to feel the pain.

- Gradually begin to imagine joining each torn scrap with strong sinewy stitches until you can envision all pieces joined into a new, durable whole.

*Alternative for groups: take turns lying on a quilt while others firmly grasp the sides, cradle and rock you, and sing lullabies to you. Be prepared for strong emotional response as deep yearning for cradling is triggered.

Fibre artist Laura Kamian of California embraces rips and tears as part of her *Torn Fabric Series*.

ACTIVITIES • REDOING

Little Dresses for Africa, initiated by Rachel O'Neill, transforms pillowcases into dresses for young girls in Africa.

Connecting globally—Try one or two of these each week this month.

▪ Change the music to rousing, marching songs.

▪ Stand erect, but not rigid, and march all around the room, breathing fully with each determined step.

▪ Imagine a roomful of others joining your march, gathering strength as you go. Imagine so many marchers that you need to move to the streets!

▪ When you feel powerfully energized, go to your closets and cedar chests to gather old, damaged, or useless garments. Spend some time taking them apart, salvaging buttons or zippers for another day.

▪ Donate the scraps to Bungong Jeumpa Creations in Banda Aceh, or to another organization that makes use of scraps.

▪ Give the good clothing that you no longer use to a shelter or a thrift store for anyone who lacks.

▪ Read about the Guatemalan weavers. As refugees from their war-torn country, their response to aid was a request for yarn so they could weave again.

▪ Get your needles out! Sewing needles, felting needles, knitting needles. Begin something new—take a class—join a guild—attend a demonstration.

▪ Research a strong person you admire. Discover what the tears and wounds have been in her life and how she has transformed them into her strength.

▪ Repeat throughout the day this quote from the resilient poet, Maya Angelou: "If you find in your heart to care for somebody else, you will have succeeded."

Rolled was created by students in Lucas Deon Spivey's quilting class for disadvantaged adults, through the Path with Art program in Washington. Another project, My Brother's Keeper, makes sleeping bags for the homeless.

RESILIENCE PROJECT • FABRIC FRAME

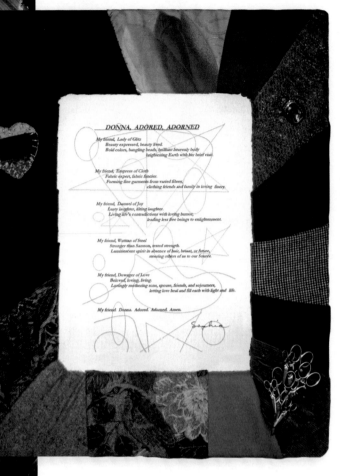

I created this wrapped frame from scraps of fabric left over from outfits Donna sewed for me, then framed the poem I read at her funeral.

• • •

I have printed and framed other inspirational messages using bits of leftover fabrics that hold meaning for me. I suggest framing your string art from the last project, or a poem, photo, or another motivational item in the wrapped frame you now create.

You will need

- Pieces of fabric from clothing, hangings, dish cloths, sewing projects, or any other source that holds symbolic meaning for you.

- Cutting on the bias increases elasticity. Each piece needs to be large enough to wrap completely around a wooden frame, with enough to tuck securely under on sides and on the back.

- A frame with a flat surface of about 1"-2" all around. A purchased frame serves well, as does one cut from heavy cardboard, or wood that is ⅛" thick.

- Scissors, needle and thread, glue (a hot-glue gun works really well).

- Notions related to the do-overs in your life—pins and jewelry, buttons, items from nature.

- Bonnie's open heart, the firm resolve of the women of Banda Aceh, and Marjorie's tenacity.

The process

- Cut swatches of each symbolic fabric about 2" in width, 4" in length.

- Turn under a small hem on the long edges, about ¼" on each; press.

- Lay the pieces on the front side of the frame, arranging them symbolically until you are satisfied. Set them aside in the arrangement so that you can now work with one piece at a time.

- Beginning at one corner, stretch the first fabric firmly across the front of the frame; turn to the back side and connect the two ends. Trim excess, check the front, then secure the piece with dots of hot glue (or firm stitches) on the back side.

- Place the next fabric just overlapping the edge of the first. Repeat the process above and continue until the entire frame is wrapped with overlapping bits of the fabrics of your life.

- Once the glue has dried, use either invisible or decorative stitches to join the fabrics on the front side.

- Arrange symbolic notions around the frame, stitching or gluing them securely.

- Place your motivational print inside the frame, secure the back, and hang it in your bathroom or beside your bed; let it remind you of the new dimensions you are always creating.

TOUGH AS LACE

The delicate work of lace-making has endured through centuries across many different cultures.

Lace. What do you think of? Most of our associations with lace are pleasant ones. Think back to your memories of lace. When did you know it was beautiful and special? Do you remember its sentimental connections—the beautiful collar on your beautiful mother's dress; the trim on your first kindergarten outfit with the twirly, whirly skirt; the fancy antimacassars (what are they?) on Grandma's plumpy chairs; the early morning spider web dotted with dewdrops; the filtered light through summer leaves; the soft spray of ocean waves?

Actually, lace-making dates back to the late 15th century and probably had a very utilitarian beginning. Lace is made by attaching threads to other threads by looping them together in some manner. Fishermen made nets to hold their catch and nomads wove net-like cloths to transport their belongings. Even lace edges on sleeves were woven to replace frayed edges.

The first well-known laces were developed in Italy and France. Needleworkers would tear threads out of woven fabrics and replace the spaces with lacy fillers. Eventually, someone thought of creating the lace without first having a fabric base. From there, creativity spawned endless variations, and, like flatbreads, most cultures have their own version of lace.

The variety of laces is endless, according to how they are made or from which culture they originated, or both. Nuns from France introduced cottage dwellers in Ireland to lace-making as a means of making a living. Arctic artisans make lace with fibres taken from the musk ox. Paraguayans make their *ñandutí,* or "spider web" lace (noted in the introduction) which is inserted into fabric for tablecloths.

The art of making lace is thriving even today as can be seen at art fairs with bobbin lace makers. The speed and dexterity they display while practicing their skills is as entertaining as any magician's sleight of hand. Crocheted and knitted laces are currently in vogue as evidenced by the abundant number of patterns and articles about them.

Jute wall hangings and plant holders were pervasive in the '60s. Cutwork, in which threads are alternately removed from and added to fabric (usually white and with even numbers of threads) is a little more traditional and was almost a lost art for awhile.

Like people who may look fragile, the strength of fibre in lace may be surprising when put to the tests life often presents.

Chapter 11

TAPESTRIES AS
INTEGRATION

Christian Prayer for Peace
Blessed are the peacemakers,
for they shall be known as the children of God.
But I say to you that hear, love your enemies,
do good to those who hate you,
Bless those who curse you, pray for those who abuse you.
To those who strike you on the cheek, offer the other also, and
from those who take away your goods, do not ask them again.
And as you wish that others would do to you, do so to them.

Hand-sewn arpilleras *depict stories and messages of social and
political significance in Chile and other South American countries.*

TAPESTRIES AS INTEGRATION

"...Each one different from the other.
But we are entwined with one another
In one great tapestry."
—Hymn by Rosemary Crow

My son values one piece of art above all others. It is a tapestry of *Dogs Playing Poker.* He values it, I believe, because of the ironic humor expressed, the kind of humor Andy lives. In a sense, it is a tapestry of his life as he joins in playful relationship with his buddies, juggles gender roles, and gambles with choices. He did not create it, but he certainly resonates with the artist.

The hand-stitched Hmong tapestry on the wall of my studio depicts the animals and plants of Southeast Asia. It tells the story of a culture connected to the natural environment where all living creatures are seen as imbued with spirit. A collectivistic culture, it is fitting that a representative Hmong tapestry is one of community, not of individuality.

Throughout centuries, people have told their individual and collective stories in the flat cloth of tapestry. Woven, appliquéd, stitched, waxed, and quilted tales of cultures and of families become an historical legacy.

Shimmering silk from Thailand depicts the villagers' lives, temples, and water buffalo side by side. Gray rough threads defining a family of old Norwegians sitting at table, praying, hung on Aunt Caroline's wall. Jan's gallery displays Inuit weavings focused on the harsh environment of arctic living. Embroidered pictures of the universe on organdy are done by Australian Jessica Rankin, while Belkis Balpinar of Turkey expresses her political views through the *kilims* she weaves. In Chile and Peru, women not only created detailed hand-sewn *arpilleras*, pictures of life in their shantytowns, but managed to stitch messages into their creations for their loved ones in prison cells.

We are all tapestries, part of a cosmic textile. Our tapestry is dynamic, constantly evolving, multidimensional. From the strings that collapse the wave of potentiality creating DNA threads braided together to

Hmong tapestry, left. Chilean *arpillera*, above, and Inuit tapestry, below. We are all tapestries, part of the cosmic textile.

form the being that is nourished through our mother's umbilical cord, our life weaves through woof and warp, becoming a uniquely designed cloth in the fabric of the universe.

We weave our story tapestry as we move through the decades. We might tell our tale in words, chronologically, focused on the events that were significant to us, or, we might depict it in images, expressed symbolically. Telling our stories in fibres not only creates a work of art, but validates our lives. Like a painter thirsting to capture a sunrise on canvas, threads and yarns preserve our unique significance. Never complete, fibres from our story are woven into the tapestries of those with whom our lives have entwined.

As we reach the late years, we review our lives. This review may offer a sense of wholeness, a synthesis of all that has occurred, or, we may look back with a sense of regret and dissatisfaction. Erik Erikson defined this life stage as "integration versus despair." We assess whether or not we have lived congruently, honoring our true essence rather than shrinking in fear and simply going along with whatever agenda the world sets for us.

Throughout the chapters, I have shared stories of my life tapestry, woven into threads of others. No true integration of my life could occur without Sophia, my inner essence, my alter ego, my guide. Jung might call her my shadow, the "Not-Me" aspects of self we deny or reject as we develop our personality. At some point in our lives, these shadow aspects cry out to be reclaimed, integrated into our wholeness.

They can be negative characteristics, difficult to own, but they can also be exciting, motivating characteristics; either way, integration requires that we reclaim them.

My relationship to Sophia manifested some years ago when I woke from a dream, threw off the covers, and felt my body stretching in soaring ballerina arches. The name, "Sophia," seemed to be whispering in the sweet summer air, calling me to listen.

I have been listening since. I call on her when I need

confidence or courage, creativity or inspiration. She is the tension of the opposites. She is my dancer. Sophia is juicy. Karen is responsible, subdued, and reticent. Jill Bolte Taylor would probably define these as left- and right-brain hemisphere personalities.

Sophia always responds. She has allowed my external professional Karen to perform the lead character in a play, to dance wildly when music summons, to speak before large audiences, and to laugh with abandon on the swings of a playground at midnight. Sophia wears flowing fuchsia gowns and walks barefoot in the middle of the winter. Karen prefers proper professorial tweeds and sensible shoes.

Integrating Sophia with Karen is essential to wholeness, to authentic living. Neither is more important than the other. They are both "Me."

I believe each person has a "Sophia" within. She represents the whisperings of our essence, that true Self that is so often silenced during childhood in order to have our needs for love, belonging, and approval met. But, she tires of silence. She speaks most loudly through life's traumas, urging us to listen to the wisdom within, and to honor that wisdom. We frequently ignore her, sacrificing the élan of freedom to maintain the roles and rules around which we have wrapped our lives.

Monica's tapestry demonstrates. My client Monica came to therapy in the midst of a devastating divorce, despairing the totality of her life. Her 30-year marriage had disintegrated just after the children had all been launched into the world. She had not pursued her own calling, in fact believed she had none. Instead, she was driven to be the "perfect" wife and mother, molding her identity into these roles. Fortunately, she loved to weave. This became her vehicle for integration.

Together, we processed Monica's life story; following each session, Monica would go home to weave those aspects of her life. Representing her childhood years as the daughter of a demanding, striving mother and a docile, passive father, Monica wove reds and oranges and red-violet fringed yarns of synthetic fibres, with images of flames emitting from the beak

Freydoon Rassouli's *Minstrel of Souls* painting seems to emanate Sophia spirit. In Christian literature, Sophia represents the divine feminine, Lady Wisdom.

of a firebird, sending sparks onto cowering chicks in the nest. Off in the distance, in pale violet, the father bird could barely be seen.

When she brought this to a session, Monica raged. Her denied anger could no longer be repressed. Finally naming it to herself, Monica began to channel its energy into positive avenues; vacuuming provided a productive physical activity during which she would vocalize the fears and hurts she felt. Needle felting was a less physical, yet satisfying, release as Monica poked with vigor the strands of wool in project after project.

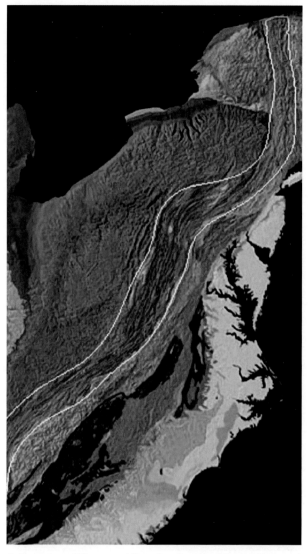

A Tapestry of Time and Terrain, Appalachian Valley and Ridge, from the USGS digital tapestry, unites two fields: geology and topography.

As she traced her school years, Monica wove tight stitches in royal blue and shades of teal, with a white slate marked "A" held by a thin figure in black and white, stiff and formal, telling of the perfectionism she demanded of herself. She talked of striving in order to quiet her mother's criticism as well as attempting to gain love from her barely-present father. Her striving continued into every arena of her life, including her body image, which erupted into anorexia in adolescence. While explaining this, Monica spoke flatly, with little emotion. As she recognized the connection to her repressed rage, she decided to take a class in expressive dance; this freedom of movement allowed a loosening of constraints, physical and emotional.

Next Monica wove five small figures in a straight line using precise, tight stitches of lime green, yellow, and orange, disconnected from one another. This portion represented her "perfect" life with her children and husband. It lacked authentic intimacy.

Monica wept as she shared this with me. Her grief was deep. She knew that she could not reclaim the years lost, the opportunities for intimate connection with those she most loved. Monica was about to rip it out. I stopped her. Explaining the need for integration of all aspects of our being, I suggested that each of these layers is, indeed, a part of Monica's life tapestry. We cannot erase what has happened in our lives, but we can claim it as an opportunity to grow from each experience, no matter how painful.

Monica began to see the possibility now before her to weave another layer, one that could be her own vision of life as she would choose to live it. I encouraged Monica to continue her tapestry.

We worked together. During sessions, we did guided imagery and relaxation exercises. On her own, Monica meditated, listening for her own "Sophia" whisperings.

She learned to live more fully in the moment, not focused on the past or the future.

She did forgiveness exercises regarding her parents, her ex, and herself in therapy. She reframed negative beliefs. Monica joined a support group for divorced and separated people where she practiced authentic sharing of herself. Monica also joined a weavers' guild where she developed friendships and intentionally showed imperfect projects to the others. She began to laugh when she made mistakes, sometimes saying aloud, "To err is human."

We worked on body image. Monica began practicing yoga instead of excessive, punitive exercise.

Spending time with her grown children now included trips to an amusement park, building sand castles at the beach, and braiding dandelions into chains while talking and listening and learning to love in that moment. No stiff dinners at perfect tables.

"...like the threads that form the woof and the warp of a single woven tapestry. To experience each strand is to experience its interweaving, which is to ultimately experience the entire tapestry."
—Uma Silbey, *Enlightenment on the Run*

During this phase, Monica did not bring any of her weaving to our sessions. I assumed she had given it up. Yet, when we discussed concluding our work together because she was enjoying her life and had recovered in large part from her divorce, Monica insisted that she needed another month.

When she came in at the end of that month, she carried a large rolled package and wore a smile of great anticipation.

Note the intentional, "Persian flaw" in rug.

She unfurled the roll and held up a completed tapestry: the bottom layers I had seen, but the last most animated one consisted of all the colors of the previous layers, woven in soft cotton, overlaid with fine silk threads depicting birds and flowers and trees and ladybugs, a stream flowing through. Monica choked when she said that this layer was about joy and "going with the flow," appreciating the beauty of all that was in her life.

She showed me an intentional error, known as a "Persian flaw," having learned from indigenous weavers this symbol of human imperfection. We both wiped tears. I encouraged Monica to hang her tapestry where she could visit it, even add to it when the next phase of her life required additional layers. We parted.

A few years later, I wandered into a gallery in a town near Monica's home. There was an exhibit of fibre art. As I browsed, I noticed a display of woven tapestries off to one side. I moved close to examine the fine work. In tiny letters at the bottom of each artful piece was a signature, "Monica." I picked up a small brochure beside the work; there was her full name and a schedule of other exhibits featuring her work.

Lovers, a woven tapestry by artist Ulrika Leander of Maryland. At left, the intentional flaw, by a different weaver, is the five-legged horse.

I examined the hangings again. Sure enough, each one, though superbly woven, included an obvious missed thread, a loosened loop, or a fibre unmatched with the others. Monica clearly had integrated her "Sophia," had reclaimed her imperfections, and was weaving them into tremendous works of art. I trust her life tapestry continues to evolve and that she continues to integrate the struggles and the triumphs into the whole.

I ponder the idea of a world tapestry. An inclusive work. All cultures, all creeds, all ways of life. Each contributing a unique dimension.

THREADS FOR THOUGHT

•According to Carl Rogers, Ph.D., humans have an "organismic valuing mechanism" that will steer us in the direction of right choices for our individual lives *if* we listen and heed the messages.

•Elisabeth Kubler-Ross, M.D., renowned author of the definitive book, *On Death and Dying,* emphasizes the importance of living fully, of responding to our "Sophia whisperings" such that we live passionately, doing what we love to do.

Detail from an *arpillera*

•One of the satisfactions of aging is the capacity to step back, to view one's life tapestry from a distance, and to see the entwining of the threads that, at the time of occurrence, seemed separate and disparate.

•Reviewing one's life offers the perspective often necessary to realize the gift in the hard times, the challenges that are opportunities for growth and connection.

•The ability to integrate the wounds, tears, and rips of one's life with the achievements, celebrations, and peak moments allows a sense of completion, a totality to all. Those who work with end-of-life issues recognize this process as critical to a peaceful acceptance of one's mortality.

•Robert N. Butler, M.D., president of the International Longevity Center in New York, identified the importance of reminiscence and life review, suggesting that the process, in fact, offers opportunity for reconciliation with disparate aspects of one's being and life.

•Being a listener for someone's life story is a gift of integration to that person and to self as witness, as is the assisting of someone in representational storytelling.

•Telling those stories repeatedly gives witness to the struggles and triumphs of individuals and of cultures.

•How will our lives be different when we respect each person's story as significantly contributing to the tapestry of the whole?

•How will our lives be different when our culture encourages slow, mindful attention to one another and to the environment?

•How will our lives be different when the last stages of life are seen as rich with opportunity to share the wisdom of life lived as well as to complete the cycle of that life?

INTEGRATIVE ACTIVITIES

Tapestry artist Ulrika Leander relaxes upon skeins of yarns, surrounded by the warp and weft of her creative life.

"When we are mindful, deeply in touch with the present moment, our understanding of what is going on deepens and we begin to be filled with acceptance, joy, peace, and love."
—Thich Nhat Hanh

Connecting within—

- Surround yourself with all those items selected in the first activity of "Webs." Touch each item, sniff each item, zoom your vision into the details of each item.

- Stand tall, surrounded by fibre work that connects you interpersonally, intergenerationally, and interculturally. Breathe in gratitude, exhale with a smile.

- Breathe in awareness of the sources of these fibres— the animals, the plants, and the synthetic substances creatively combined. Breathe in appreciation, breathe out compassion for those who contributed.

- Breathe in three deep belly breaths as you allow your mind's eye to scan all cells, tissues, and organs of your own fibre, your body. Exhale fully, feeling the interdependence of your body with the external world.

- Ask a silent question regarding your "calling," your purpose.

- Sit quietly, surrounded by fibre, in touch with fibre, riding the wave of rhythmic breath. Listen intently for your "Sophia whisperings," without expectation of a specific answer at this time.

- When you are ready, write the question that you asked in your journal. Then, without pausing, without censorship, write three pages in response. *None* of it has to make sense; no judgment, just allowing.

- Create a timeline of your life, recording in brief notes the most significant events of your life, positive and negative. Imagine a symbol in fibre or color that might represent each of the most impactful of these.

- Using a highlighter, overlay the significant cultural and global events on your individual timeline. Again, imagine a symbol representing each of these.

- Visualize a tapestry of your life, your culture, your place in the universe.

- Ask someone you trust to listen to your story.

Market day at Bac Ha Market in Vietnam. The Flower Hmong who gather there are known for their rich textiles.

Expanding connections—Try one of these each week this month.

- Volunteer to listen to the life story of the person who listened for you. When you do so, do not interject your own story; simply listen.

- Visit a hospital or nursing home, an infirm neighbor, or a hospice center. Volunteer to be a listener. Sit and hear the stories of others, validating their lives by your presence.

- To learn more about the tapestries of Turkey and how you might support the women who create them, visit the website www.handsonhips.org.

- Watch the Canadian documentary *Threads of Hope*, narrated by Donald Sutherland, to witness the powerful story of Chilean women who used their *arpilleras* in the struggle to find their husbands, sons, and fathers who had disappeared. Also visit the website of Education and More, for stories of Guatemalan weaving cooperatives.

- Read about Inuit art, then visit a shop or gallery displaying Inuit tapestries. Or, research the fibre art of any indigenous culture; then find an exhibit to view (virtual viewing works!).

My friend Judie Johnson, a basket maker, shared with me these beautiful fabrics from Bhutan.

INTEGRATION PROJECT • COLLAGE

This collage will be your tapestry, representing the integration of many dimensions of your life.

You will need

- A variety of fabric swatches in many colors and textures.

- One background piece of fabric, 17"x17" or of your choosing.

- A second piece of fabric exactly the same size.

- Needles, threads, and scissors.

The process

- Having done the visioning process in Integrative Activities, this process aims to capture symbolically your story in its totality.

- Review your time line; select a fabric that represents the color and texture of each significant event. (Leftover fabric from my wedding dress is my base, a feedsack napkin is my childhood, etc.)

- Trim each swatch into a shape that represents that aspect of your life. Do the same with cultural and global events. (Torn terry cloth represents "war," into which I was born, for example.)

- Arrange, overlay, design these swatches on the background until you have a sense that your collage integrates all the meaningful layers. Pin them in place.

- Then, over time, hand stitch them to one another and to the background fabric until all is secure.

- Embroider words, phrases, additional images as intuition guides you. (For example, I chose "war," "dance," "green," as influences in my life.)

- When your tapestry/collage is complete, press it neatly.

- Placing right sides of the collage and the additional piece of fabric together, pin together on three sides. Stitch firmly in place, by machine or by hand, using small, firm stitches.

- Turn it to the right side, and insert a prepared 16"x16" pillow, or stuff with appropriate filler.

- Hand stitch the fourth side firmly in place.

- Place your tapestry collage pillow at the head of your bed. Visit it daily as you integrate all aspects of your being.

- Gather a group of friends and share your life stories through the collages.

It is important that we tell our story, but not remain stuck in our story; we can rip out, reweave, and create new chapters to our stories when the old ones no longer serve us.

• • •

Reconciliation is a process of reweaving new relationships with those from whom we have been estranged.

• • •

Forgiveness is not a requirement, but a gift we give ourselves in order to reclaim the enormous energy invested in sustaining resentment.

DOLLS, DOLLS, DOLLS!

Replicas of human beings. Universal play things. Collectors' items. Storytellers. Meaningful tapestries of life. Dolls, manufactured and homespun, permeate every culture across the globe and through the ages. Something in our nature longs to duplicate our form and express our humanness in the form of dolls. From primitive carved sticks to elaborately molded and adorned princess figures, dolls allow us to tell our stories and imagine new ones. They allow emotional expression and imaginative play. They stand at attention on collectors' shelves and are cuddled snuggly in little ones' beds. And, they make wonderful gifts. Perhaps nothing represents integration as aptly as dolls.

A favorite childhood book, *The Surprise Doll* by Morrell Gipson, tells the story of little Mary, whose father traveled the globe. From each culture visited, Mary's father brought back a doll for her. Though Mary loved her six dolls, she wanted something more. Independently, she took them to a wise toymaker who recognized our universality and created a seventh doll. This doll included some characteristic of each of the six and looked exactly like Mary. This "surprise doll" represented Mary's plurality as well as her individuality, her integration.

Fibre artists create dolls to capture personality; Julie, for instance, created a doll with six legs, each wearing a spectacular pair of shoes for her sister with a shoe fetish. Andrea made a doll with moss hair and pine-cone feet to represent her naturalist aunt. Joann made dolls to amuse her grandchildren and the kids in the neighborhood. They evolved into whimsical characters with fascinating stories that came to Joann as she created them.

Dolls are for universal play and healing.

Her studio cabinet is filled with her creations. There's a "brat with attitude," who won't put on her t-shirt. A "goodness doll" has scouring-pad hair and a pretty body made out of a cone; she has no legs. "Nada" has gold tights and flaming red, fur hair. There is a whole world inside that cabinet.

Therapists facilitate clients in creating dolls to represent wounds as well as strengths; one woman, for example, stitched a heart with a scar over it and a bright sunburst over her solar plexus to show the strength she has developed after painful losses. Social workers use anatomically correct dolls to assist children in talking about abuse. Some therapists employ "Dammit Dolls" for cathartic expression of anger.

Retired and seeking more purpose in her life, Lynn Zwerling now teaches soon-to-be-released prisoners to knit and crochet. The men meet in weekly, two-hour sessions to create "comfort dolls" that they name after the prison guards. The men base the names on the hair of the doll and find humor in representing their guards. The dolls are donated to children who have been through trauma.

"Knitting gives you anger management, goal orientation, self-confidence, pride…all the things that you need to know in life in order to be successful," says Zwerling.

Stitching dolls for children in Chiapas brought together people in our community on cold winter days; we laughed and talked and created with purpose. Our group included elders from the care center and youth from a Scout troop. Compassion, creativity, contribution, cooperation, connection. Hmmm… Integration. Dolls.

Chapter 12

CELEBRATING
THE FABRIC OF LIFE

Zoroastrian Prayer for Peace
We pray to God to eradicate all misery in the world:
That understanding triumph over ignorance,
That generosity triumph over indifference,
That trust triumph over contempt,
And that truth triumph over falsehood.

Veils, scarves, and fluid fabrics create this color wheel as
Dancers for Positivity *celebrate life.*

CELEBRATING THE FABRIC OF LIFE

"As soon as I started dancing, something familiar inside woke up—me!"
—Karen Andes, *A Woman's Book of Power*

My ordination as a "woman of the cloth" unfolded in a dream before an altar draped with Mayan needlework.

In the distance I see an old, wise woman standing in front of a cold marble altar, draped in rich Mayan weaving. I recognize this as the church of my childhood. Incense burning, soft organ music is playing a song I remember from high school chorus, "The Lost Chord." The woman beckons me. I slowly walk the long brick aisle toward her, soon recognizing that she is my maternal grandmother, Helga. I never met her, but I know her. She crocheted the scarf I ruined at the warming house.

As I approach, she holds out a tiny, delicate, but slightly brown-with-age baptismal gown. I know that it is the gown she made for my mother. Tiny stitches apply an overlay of translucent, intricately designed lace over the bodice, while minute pearl buttons fasten the back through fine threaded loops, and a long, flowing skirt reaches far beyond the legs of any infant. I recall this dress from my mother's cedar chest. Worn by my older siblings for their baptisms, it was too aged for mine. Helga seems to want me to wear the tiny dress. I tell her it won't fit. She slips it over my head and at once it becomes a glorious bridal gown of antique lace sewn by my friend Katie, for her sister's wedding. I pause for a moment to admire its regal elegance. I protest that I am too old and too married to be a bride. As I turn from the altar, the gown transforms into a clerical vestment with a colorful scarf of many designs draped from hem to hem, each section sewn by a loved one.

I am astonished when Helga tells me that this is my ordination! "You've always appreciated fibre art; now, you are a 'woman of the cloth!' You are ordained to teach ordinary wonder!"

I laugh gleefully. As I laugh, I hear waves of laughter from behind. When I turn, we are in a ballroom with rockin' music playing; my husband, my children, my siblings, my friends, and soul mates from around the globe are dancing in celebratory rhythm, laughing with abandon. We all laugh and laugh and laugh as we dance and dance. Among the dancers is Donna, waving the prayer shawl that draped her shoulders in dying. We dance together, giggling. Marie whispers to me, "I thought she was dead?" I answer, "She is, she's just here for this celebration!" And we go on dancing and laughing.

I wake with a smile and hang onto the dream, so filled with symbolic meaning and joy. I hear the sound of spring waxwings gobbling the last of the fermented ash berries on the tree outside my slightly open window. A crisp breeze caresses my cold cheeks as I snuggle deeply into the flannel covers. Freshness fills my being and I feel as though every photon in each cell of my body is alive and awake. I reach for my journal to capture this dream before shifting into ordinary consciousness. I must call Sophie to walk me through her dream analysis process. Yet, I know the symbolism already.

Rituals serve a vital purpose for us. Rituals in all cultures and religious traditions mark significant life passages, allowing us to come together as family and community, validating the importance of the event. Rituals connect the present participants with all those who have carried out a specific observance before.

Most passages are celebrated with specific garments indicative of the event, calling on the highest skill of fibre artists, humble and grand. The opulent gowns of royal coronations, often stitched with metallic threads and accented with jewels, celebrate the transition to a new monarchy. African royalty wear layers of symbolic *kente* cloth for which they are renowned, the colors imbued with meaning. Michelle Obama's gown selection for her husband's inauguration instantly made famous its designer.

In the Christian tradition, the baptismal ritual not only marks the welcoming of a child into the church community, but declares the importance of support from others in helping the parents raise the child. It expresses the hope of a new life. The long flowing baptismal gown of my mother's day has been replaced by simpler clothing for the baby, usually in white or delicate pastels.

The observance of Bar or Bat Mitzvah in the Jewish faith signals the "coming of age" of an adolescent who often wears a *tallit*, or prayer shawl. A vision quest was a marker of emerging adulthood in the Native American tradition, requiring minimal clothing, but tribal ceremonies often include elaborate garments of animal hide, symbolically accented with feathers, beads, and jingling shells. In the royal palace of Bangkok, Thailand, the golden Buddha's garb is changed according to the season. Celebration of the New Year in the Hmong culture includes a time of "tossing ball"

In my dream, soul mates from around the world join me in celebratory dance.

in which young men and women are able to communicate with potential marriage partners wearing ornate traditional Hmong costumes such as that worn by Ying when she spoke at Anna's school.

Every two years we feast our eyes on ceremonial garb as the world celebrates the Olympics. Citizens of the host country don traditional costumes for an elaborate opening ceremony. As host, China enlisted 15,000 performers regaled in a breathtaking array of costumes representing eras of Chinese history. The competing athletes parade the colors of their nations. Competition and commonality are celebrated in the enduring ritual of the Olympic games.

All cultures have wedding and funeral rituals. Wedding gowns cover the spectrum in color and design, each marking the joining of lives. The creation of a wedding gown can also build relationship. The fiancé of Mary's daughter sewed her gown, deepening a bond of trust with each careful stitch. The gown Katie sewed for her sister remains a symbol of a time in which they were most connected. Alexa's red silk gown had been sewn and worn by her mother in a very traditional Chinese wedding on another continent in another time, now deeply bonding generations.

Some life transitions lack ritual. Neither menarche nor menopause is celebrated formally in most cultures. The launching of the last child, creating the "empty nest" syndrome, leaves parents struggling with ambivalent feelings of loss and excitement, yet without a ceremony to assist the process. Divorce is seldom marked with anything but a court paper and perhaps a drink with a friend, though the greeting card industry has responded. Adoption lacks ritual observance. And, though clergy have an ordination ritual, most do not. Yet, each of us is, indeed, "ordained" to some life purpose.

Discovering that purpose, that "calling" requires presence, listening to those sweet whisperings in our soul, paying attention to what ignites our passion. Some people seem to know and heed the calling early in life, while others wake to it much later. Some never listen, choosing instead to contort themselves to fill roles that do not feed their souls, do not lead them to thrive. Angst, not peace, results from living inauthentic lives. No matter how humble the calling, authentic living, in concert with true Self, gives reason for great celebration.

I ponder, then, the message in my dream. "You are ordained to teach ordinary wonder," Helga said. The call to teach has shown up in many ways throughout my life. My first career was teaching elementary school. Later, a strong pull to study applied psychology was realized when I returned to graduate school.

Counseling is teaching of another variety. Later, I combined these threads by teaching psychology at the university. Yet, this idea of teaching "ordinary wonder" is curious.

I sit with my musings and my journal. Suddenly, the message is clear. Wondrous fibres—ordinary, extraordinary, ancient, and completely modern fibres! Viewing with awe the intricate design of a spider's web glistening in the dew, touching the musty softness of newly shorn wool, watching the deft fingers of an indigenous woman weave a garment to feed her family, dancing with fluid silk undulating to an orchestra's waves of sound, simple fibres create connection and beauty. This is what I am ordained to teach.

This purpose has been gestating for a decade, forming and re-forming, twisting into meaning, just like crocheting with simple yarns, until, finally, the piece is birthed. This is my new classroom.

I decide to create a ritual in celebration. A trip to the bargain table at the closest fabric store yields exactly what I need. I check out a local park for space and reserve it for my birthday in a month. I enlist my talented sister-in-law to weave fibre invitations, a specialty of hers. I get busy with planning.

The day dawns uncertainly. Gray clouds create a mystical haze. Rain may visit my ordination ceremony. I remind myself to celebrate the gift of precipitation.

I dress for the occasion with intention, slipping into a blue dress made by my eldest daughter when she was an adolescent. I belt it with finger weaving done by my second daughter, then pin a crocheted handkerchief of my mother's to the waist, add my wedding pearls, drape a fabulous "hyperbolic" scarf knit by Anna, and finish with my favorite "Donna" watch. I pack my glasses and other necessities in the burlap bag my little son created. I look eccentric. I like that.

The park is empty when I arrive. Draping tables with Jan's batik cloths, arranging decorative scarves, poking in fragrant sprigs of lilac, and setting up colorful platters of food, accompanied only by the sounds of birds chirping and red squirrels chattering, I savor the gift of solitude to listen to Sophia whisperings on this,

My mother in a hand-sewn confirmation dress in 1918. Weaving ritual at my ordination to teach ordinary wonder.

the celebration of my birth and ordination in one. I smile. Guests arrive.

Guests arrive. I giggle. Obviously, my loved ones get it! They, too, have been willing to be present to the day smacking of symbolic meaning. Sophie wears a shawl that she has woven of Igor's heavy gray fleece. She contributes a huge vat of her savory lentil soup to the feast. Iris arrives, operatic voice singing "Happy Birthday" as she emerges from her car in a crocheted sweater of swirls and spirals, pinks, lavenders, reds.

Anna comes with felted flower brooches adorning a felted hat, while Arlene wears the dress she made from the purple Chinese silk Beth and I gave her. Madge wears her "patches pants." Marie is draped in her lustful scarf, arm linked with her new beau. Even Bob has wrapped a certain short, red, hand-knit muffler around his neck. Andy arrives with a grinning Abbie in a brocaded dress from Chiapas. Jake's shy, "Happy birthday, Gamma" warms the chilly day.

Finally, all have gathered. Katie has conspired with me to lead the ceremony. In fact, she surprises me by donning her own "clerical scarf" constructed of cream-colored textured weavings she has created.

In authentic ministerial style, she welcomes the

crowd, then directs them to form a square, with six people lining each side. From the box beside her, Katie extracts 12 pieces of fabric, my purchases from the bargain table, each color of the rainbow in three-yard lengths. As she hands an end to the six on one side and instructs those opposite to take the other end, stretching the fabric taut, Katie asks participants to think deeply about ordinary wonders that contribute to peace, then to designate that meaning to each "thread."

After a few silent moments, Madge shouts, "Blue is the beauty of sky and water!"

Another moment, then simultaneous shouts:

"Orange is for autumn leaves, and for the warmth of fires."

"Yellow for the courage of the poor as well as the innocence of daffodils!"

"Ducks with heads of brilliant green like the trees in springtime."

"How about purple for spiritual passion?"

"And, kindness seems to me to be a deep, burnt orange...."

The warp is set.

Now Katie distributes an end of the remaining six

Prayer flags flutter across a stream on the Annapurna Trail in Nepal. The flags, usually arranged in the same color sequence, carry blessings of peace and prosperity.

the threads, then to lean back with heels planted in the earth. "Feel our entwined strength," she exclaims. "Witness our united beauty! Experience the peace we have created."

A wave of extraordinary peace envelops the entire park.

After a few soulful, silent moments, I crank the volume of Mariah Carey tunes from my "boom box." Katie encourages the group to dance, and soon the huge fabric is surging to the rhythms as the group finds its harmony in movement.

Perhaps the aroma of the spring lilacs touches my brain, for suddenly, without thought, I grab the ends of my spiral scarf and spin wildly—almost weightlessly—around the group weaving. Sophia soars.

I know that this diverse group, now united, will respond to the next part of my celebration—gifts! I had specifically requested special gifts on my invitation—handmade fibre creations that will warm and delight people at a nearby shelter.

lengths to the third side of the square and asks the opposite six to become the shuttle. Taking the loose end of the woof threads, they walk over and under as the warp people assist by raising and lowering their taut "strings." The guys protest that "this is ridiculous!" Some get all mixed up and mess up the "warp and woof" pattern. But, Katie redirects and commands. They cooperate with humor.

As they proceed, enthusiasm builds. The tertiary colors are named symbolically; teal is "wisdom," lavender becomes "originality," and lime is declared "seasoning." One by one, they step gingerly in and out, laughing at the challenge to keep straight which is next. When all six are finally on their original side, Katie instructs everyone to stretch the fabric "threads" to full width and full length. Audible exclamations of wonder escape. The room-sized weaving is awesome!

Assertively, Katie instructs the group to grasp firmly

Katie now asks that the gifts be placed in the center of the fabric just woven. Fleece mittens and hats join small sweaters, woven shawls, a colorful afghan, and two quilted vests. Katie has crocheted a beautiful mauve blanket. Several pastel baby booties land atop the rest. Andy lifts Abbie as she throws on felted pieces that her stepmother, Erika, helped her attach to fleece fabric, creating a lap robe. Hand-sewn dolls spring forth. And scarves. Silk ones, long ones, colorful ones, cozy ones. I throw on a pair of imperfect, but warm, woolen slippers, almost equal in size. The fabric is weighted with gifts.

I thank them all for this act of ordinary wonder. I do feel ordained.

Fulfilling an impulse perhaps inspired by her ceremonial garb, Katie offers this benediction: "Go in peace. Mend the world."

THREADS FOR THOUGHT

•In *Natural Grace*, Matthew Fox and Rupert Sheldrake discuss, among other things, the importance of ritual as related to morphic resonance, the connection of the past with present and future, in repeatedly celebrating significant events.

•In his books, *Learned Optimism* and *Authentic Happiness*, Martin Seligman explains the importance of attitude, gratitude, and positive reframing of life's events in order to experience contentment.

Peace symbol quilt by Mary Smith

•Simplifying concepts helps us to understand and internalize, according to the principle of "Occam's razor." Ceremony is an avenue to simplification.

•Ceremony assists in adjusting to change, positive and negative, in our lives.

•The importance of witnessing for another is an aspect of celebration.

•David I. Kertzer's book, *Ritual, Politics, and Power,* discusses the vital role of ritual, including symbolic clothing, in the powerful world of politics.

•Ceremonial celebration often involves many feminine characteristics—care, compassion, connection, creativity, and contribution.

•Ceremonial celebration also can involve the masculine characteristics of assertion, autonomy, and action.

•Ceremonial celebration gives occasion for the balancing of art, spirituality, and science.

•How will our lives be different when we establish ritual celebrations for those passages that go unmarked, yet involve great emotional turmoil?

•How will our lives be different when we establish a Department of Peace at every level of government, initiating it with great pomp and circumstance?

•How will our lives be different when we establish a celebration of all life across the globe?

CELEBRATION ACTIVITIES

"Let us be fully present to the beautiful moment that is now."
—Thich Nhat Hahn

These activities are designed to celebrate your unique contribution to the creation of peace!

Creating to essence—

- Spread a colorful bed of fabrics on the floor. Include one flowing piece with silver or gold, or other flamboyant aspect to it. Stand in the middle.

- Presence. Breathe in the beautiful moment that is now. Take six deep belly breaths, exhaling with an audible, full sigh after each.

- Hum your favorite tune while you gently massage your temples and cheeks.

- "Slap" your arms, belly, and legs awake…gently!

- Stretch every limb in long, invigorating poses.

- Now, go wild! Get silly! Grab your flowing piece of fabric and start to laugh. Begin with giggles, then laugh from your belly. Run, skip, jump, twirl around the room! Celebrate life!

- Do something outrageous today!

Dare we imagine and fully participate in the creation of one peaceful world by becoming our fullest, most passionate Selves?

Expansive connection—
Do this one time this year!

- Decide how you would like to celebrate your own "ordination." Create a ceremony. Invite others. Include contribution to the larger world.

- Determine the appropriate garb for your ceremony. Wear it with joy!

- Do it! Finish with dancing belly laughs.

Yarnstorming, or yarnbombing, has become an exuberant activity for fibre graffiti artists worldwide. "I want to reconnect the community," says fibre artist Denise Litchfield of her yarn graffiti covering this tree.

CELEBRATION PROJECT • BATIK CLOTH

Friends Bonnie Gay and Korey hold up batiks they created at a workshop Jan offered.

Creating a celebratory meditation cloth using the ancient, universal fibre art of batik, brings us full circle back to the women of Java who created my exquisite tablecloth. It is a meditative process, inviting introspection.

Merging masculine qualities of assertion, autonomy, and logic with feminine qualities of compassion, cooperation, creativity, and contribution becomes a celebration in itself.

First, check out batik online

This project will take at least three separate time periods of one to two hours each. Before proceeding, you might want to visit www.dharmatrading.com, a website with instructions, supplies, and safety tips for batiking. Browsing this site and ordering supplies is a good way to try batik if you do not have an instructor.

Another website, www.pburch.net, also has good technique instructions. You may also view a variety of Chinese batiks at www.turtleislandimports.com.

You will need

- Cotton cloth, approximately 14" x 14" square
- Synthrapol dye detergent
- Dark pencil
- Procion dyes in at least the three colors, fuschia, turquoise, and lemon yellow, plus black
- Paint brushes in a variety of sizes
- Old electric skillet, or another way of safely heating wax
- Simple wooden frames, the same size of your cloth
- Thumbtacks, to tack your cloth to the frame
- Wax to melt (paraffin and/or beeswax)
- Heavy rubber gloves
- Large container, preferably stainless steel, for black dye
- An old iron
- Layers of plain newsprint

In Mexico, we hung our cloth to dry under palms.

The process

- Tack cloth to frame. Sketch with dark pencil on your cloth a design that feels celebratory and invites color. Trace from another source or create an original design.

- Decide where, if anywhere, you want white to remain.

- Choosing old brushes that will only be used for wax, paint hot wax on those areas. This will prevent color from entering those areas. The wax should be hot enough to penetrate the fabric; if it is too cool, color will seep through.

- Now paint the remaining colors onto your design as you want them. Colors will blend as they touch; for optimal blending, wet the entire area to be painted with water before painting color. For more distinct separation of color, minimize water.

- Allow all painted fabric to dry thoroughly before waxing. You may simply air dry them, or use a hair dryer to hasten this process.

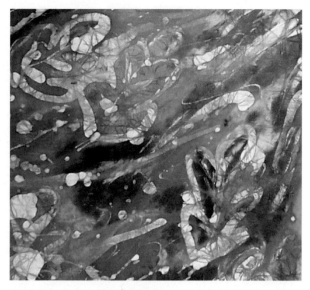

Batik by another friend, Judy.

- With the wax brush, apply hot wax to all color areas you wish to preserve. Leave unwaxed borders between sections of your design so that they can become black outlines in the final dye bath.

- Add additional color to any areas you have not waxed as you wish. Allow thorough drying time.

- Wax all additional areas you wish to remain other than black. Use a large paint brush for background waxing.

- When waxing is complete, remove cloth from frame. Crinkle cloth to allow tiny cracks in the waxed area; this allows the distinct batik effect of black dye throughout the color.

- Dip the entire cloth into a vat of black dye.

- Hang to dry.

- Once completely dry, use an old damp rag to wipe off excess black dye.

- "Sandwich" your cloth between layers of newsprint.

- Iron at a very hot temperature, melting the wax, which will be absorbed into the newsprint.

- Repeat with new layers of newsprint until most of the wax is removed.

- Wash with synthrapol dye detergent to set the colors.

- Hang on a window or with a background light to appreciate the vivid colors and design you have created.

- Use this meditation cloth as the center point of your celebratory ceremony and for your daily practice of peace.

A section of reef from Scottsdale, Arizona, a satellite of the reef project by the Institute For Figuring

HYPERBOLIC CORAL REEF PROJECT

Integration is a major theme of *Peace Fibres*. In the introduction to this book, I discuss the integration of right and left brain, masculine and feminine qualities. I emphasize the interdependence of the human with the natural world. And, in the first chapter, I introduce Dr. Daina Taimina's crocheted model of hyperbolic space. This model inspired Australian-born sisters Margaret and Christine Wertheim to adapt Dr. Taimina's techniques to develop a whole taxonomy of reef-life forms, the Hyperbolic Coral Reef Project.

The purpose of the project is to focus attention on the peril of these natural underwater wonders, endangered from human pollution. Described as "a woolly celebration of the intersection of higher geometry and feminine handicraft, and a testimony to the disappearing wonders of the marine world," this fascinating project integrates biology, mathematics, ecology, global community, and fibre work!

The two sisters enlisted their own crochet skills to initiate the reef project through the Institute For Figuring, where Margaret is director. Eventually, over 800 people, from three to 101 years in age, poked and twisted yarns to create the spectacular model, part of which was exhibited at the Smithsonian Institution and can be viewed online (www.Smithsonian.com) or in the December 2010 issue of *Smithsonian Magazine*.

Other reef projects multiplied across the world and, like life's longing to sustain itself, they continue to evolve. The vibrant, curious unseen world under the sea before our eyes; the colorless areas of bleached coral alert us to the reality of the damage we have done. This awesome project offers avenues of action to change course in service of our environment. As Wertheim says, "We humans, when we work together, can do amazing things."

This is a project in which anyone can participate. Plans for creating your own hyperbolic models are included in Dr. Taimina's book, *Crocheting Adventures with the Hyperbolic Planes,* and are available online at http://theiff.org.

Dr. Daina Taimina, teaching hyperbolic crochet at this workshop at Gallery Azur in Riga, Latvia

Graceful and expressive, this ribbon dance is a celebration in silk.

CONNECTIONS AND CELEBRATIONS

Let there be dancing!

"Dance is the hidden language of the soul," says Martha Graham. Exuberant joy just makes a body want to move. And fibres move as gracefully as our bodies, so they are the perfect accompaniment. Across the globe, throughout time, human beings entwine themselves with fluid, flowing fibres to undulate, weave, stomp, and leap in harmonious relationship with the pulses of drums, bagpipes, flutes, harps and other stringed instruments. Every culture since the dawn of humanity celebrates significant passages through dances adorned with fibres.

In China and Japan, dancers twirl long, swirling ribbons of silk as they move in concert to the music. Each movement has significance. The Chinese dance dates to dynasties thousands of years old, originally performed only for royalty. Legend has it that the silk sleeve of a dancer saved the life of the emperor; the silk ribbon dance was initiated in tribute. Many of us were privileged to view this ribbon dance during the 2008 Beijing Olympic ceremony.

Other cultures employ flowing fabrics in their celebratory dances as well. Maypole dancing, of European origin, features dancers and trees (poles) connected with long colorful ribbons. The dancers circle the tree until it is entirely wrapped in the colorful fibres. Hawaiian hula dancers and Native American grass dancers swish and sway with the long fibres of nature, while Spanish Flamenco, Latin American Salsa, and Middle Eastern belly dancing are accented with ribbons, fringes, and veils…oh, yes, veils….

The "Dance of the Seven Veils." Erotic, sensual, celebratory. Depicted in Oscar Wilde's play, the shedding of the seven veils has a variety of interpretations, from the biblical story of Salome asking for the head of John the Baptist, to the ancient myth of the Sumerian Goddess Inanna descending into the underworld in a metaphor of self-actualization. Whatever interpretation you prefer, belly dancing has become popular in the United States as a healthy, playful, and erotic expression of the feminine.

Metaphor through masks and costumes are the hallmark of dances in many cultures. Maori *Kapa Haka* dancers, African tribal dancers, and Inuit dancers create masks that depict creatures of nature or mythical characters as they act out stories of heroism, successful hunts, and interdependence with the cosmic forces.

Fluid fibres. Music. Color. Movement. Our senses. Our bodies. All peoples. The cosmos. Earth's creatures. All connected. All one. Celebrate, celebrate, celebrate. Don't sit on the sidelines; even if you have a disability that challenges you, hands or eyes can join in the movement. This is the moment we have. Pick up some fibres. Dance!

Fibre art celebrates dance in the batik from India, above, and in this batik by Suzanne Drown of Maine.

Open arms to the sky—
Art Deco, fabric sculpture by
Merilyn Thomas of Australia

AFTERTHREAD
CONNECTING THE STRINGS

A great theory of everything eluded Einstein. Not Katie. She united art, spirit, and science in one little scrunch ball.

After contacting Dr. Taimina for permission to include an image of her crocheted hyperbolic model in this book, Katie obtained the instructions for making one.

Into that scientific model, Katie wrapped her loving friendship and created an object of beauty. The true, the good, and the beautiful entwined through her fingers as they stitched and poked and looped.

I squealed in delight when I opened the small square box on my birthday! Katie's scrunch ball embodies the thesis of *Peace Fibres*.

Joining, connecting, unifying. An image. An intention. One tiny sizzling thread joins another, then another, until a form emerges. A canvas. A garment. A scrunch ball. Making beauty. Warming. Comforting. Inspiring connection. Inviting contribution. Instilling peace. Fibre work is both metaphor and manifestation of harmonious relationship to self, others, and the larger world.

Greg shares the calming effect of his knitting; Virginia exclaims the revelatory nature of a self-portrait doll; John shares the connection his aunt's knitting provided his family; Jill tells her story of emotional healing through quilting. Mention fibres and stories spin. From indigenous villages to intimate relationships, the eternal thread that joins us twists and loops, expanding, ever expanding, our commonality and connection across generations and cultures. *Ñandutí* lace.

Imagine if politicians and corporate leaders, economists and brokers, professors and physicians, janitors and servers, mothers and children all began their day with a quiet focus in spinning, knitting, or stitching. What if organizations and families resolved their conflicts as they worked together on a quilt for a shelter? What if athletes and artists pooled their talents to create strong, decorative gear for the disabled? The imaginings are endless. Positive global warming. Fibres allow peace within, peaceful relationship.

Fibre work is not a panacea. Peace is complicated. Like the slow-foods movement, working with fibres slows us down instead of propelling us headlong into the world. Peace begins with the individual. Fibres offer an organic beginning at the level of substance, creating a strong, flexible, world fabric. Anyone and everyone can weave threads of peace.

Let there be peace on Earth. Let it begin with me.

REFERENCES, RESOURCES, CREDITS

PRODUCTION CREDITS
Book design by Maryl Skinner and Denny FitzPatrick of M Graphic
   Design, mgraphic@boreal.org. Grand Marais, Minnesota.
Images not credited below were photographed by Maryl Skinner,
   Denny FitzPatrick, or Karen Lohn. All artists and photographers
   retain the copyright to their own work.
Printed in Canada by Friesens.

FRONT COVER
Beaded felting by Linda Bauer,
   www.ravensbeakdesign.com. Minnesota.
Prayer flags at base camp in Nepal courtesy of Cosley and Houston
   Alpine Guides at www.cosleyhouston.com. France.
Chilean *arpillera* courtesy of Margaret Snook,
   www.cachandochile.com. Chile.
Sunshine quilt square courtesy of Karen Musgrave,
   www.connectionsbykaren.blogspot.com. Illinois.
Felted heart by Mary Fechner. Michigan.

BACK COVER
Quilted journal by Marci Glenn at Simply Artistic Pleasures,
   www.marciglenn.wordpress.com. Oregon.
Rolled by students of Path with Art in collaboration with Recovery
   Café, courtesy of teaching artist, Lucas Deon Spivey,
   www.pathwithart.org. Washington.
Ñandutí lace courtesy of Sergio at Gabinete de Curiosidades,
   http://www.gabinetedecuriosidades.com.br. São Paulo, Brazil.
Dancing brooch courtesy of Sandra Haff and the artists at
   I Love a Parade: Art Created by Your Homeless Neighbors,
   www.iloveaparade.org. Minneapolis, Minnesota.

ACKNOWLEDGMENTS
Gratitude symbol courtesy of Stacey Robyn, www.gogratitude.com.

INTRODUCTION
Credits
3 Quotation. Words of Etty Hillesum from: Gaarlandt, Jan G. Etty
   Hillesum: *An Interrupted Life: the Diaries, 1941-1943.* Henry Holt
   & Company, Inc. N.Y. 1996.
4 Quotation. Dr. Jill Bolte Taylor. *My Stroke of Insight: A Brain Scientist's Personal Journey.* Penguin Group. NY. 2006.

Images
3 Peruvian Women's Cooperative courtesy of Annie O. Waterman,
   www.annieoboutique.com. Colorado.
3 Cooperative Artisanale Feminine des Boutons en Soie 'Cerises.' In
   Almis Guigou, Sefrou Province, Morocco. Used by permission of
   Amina Yabis and Jonathan Santeliz. Morocco.
4 Andi, *Saori* weaving courtesy of photographer Terri Bibby,
   www.saorisaltspring.com. British Columbia.
5 *Ñandutí* lace courtesy of Sergio at Gabinete de Curiosidades,
   http://www.gabinetedecuriosidades.com.br. São Paulo, Brazil.

CHAPTER 1 — WEBS OF CONNECTION
Credits
14 Quotation. Thich Nhat Hanh. *The Blooming of a Lotus: Guided
   Meditation for Achieving the Miracle of Mindfulness.* Beacon
   Press. Boston. 1993.

Images
6 Border from fabric courtesy of Whitney Taylor,
   www.littlemangoimports.com. Colorado.
6 Spider web photo on Isle Royale, Michigan.
8 Thai woman weaving. Northern Thailand.
10 Batik women. Jojakarta, Java.
11 APEC leaders courtesy of *The Jakarta Post.* Jakarta, Indonesia.
   Photographer Kosasih Derajat. Indonesia.
12 Silkworms and mulberry leaves in Suzhou, China. 12-13-06.
   Author Magnus Lewan. Public Domain. Wikimedia Commons.
12 Golden orb spider courtesy of photographer Michael Francisco.
   Louisiana.
13 Model of hyperbolic space courtesy of Dr. Daina Taimina, Cornell
   University. New York.
14 Fabric figure sculpture courtesy of Jo,
   www.nzjo.wordpress.com. New Zealand.
15 Nootka woman wrapped in cedar bark. Photographer Edward S.
   Curtis. Courtesy of Northwestern University. Illinois.
16 Worry yarn photographed by Shannon Geddes,
   www.knitmeariver.blogspot.com. North Carolina.
17 Sewing threads by Petr Kratochvil, http://www.publicdomain-
   pictures.net/view-image.php?image=2627&picture=sewing-
   threads>Sewing Threads</a> by Petr Kratochvil.

Books
The following are background texts for the various dimensions of the
thesis of *Peace Fibres*:
Bolen, M.D., Jean Shinoda. *Goddesses in Every Woman: A New Psy-
   chology of Women.* Harper and Row. NY. 1984
Capra, Fritjof. *The Tao of Physics: An Exploration of the Parallels
   Between Modern Physics and Eastern Mysticism.* Shambhala Pub-
   lications. Boston, MA. 1991.
Eisler, Riane. *The Chalice and the Blade: Our History, Our Future.*
   Harper Collins. San Francisco, CA. 1987.
Gilligan, Carol. *In a Different Voice: Psychological Theory and
   Women's Development.* Harvard University Press. Cambridge, MA.
   1982.
Maslow, Abraham H. *Motivation and Personality.* Harper and Row,
   NY. 1970.
Moore, Thomas. *Care of the Soul: A Guide for Cultivating Depth and
   Sacredness in Everyday Life.* Harper Perennial. 1992.
Musgrove, Margaret, illustrated by Julia Cairns. *The Spider Weaver: A
   Legend of Kente Cloth.* Blue Sky Press. 2001. (Ages 4-10 years)
Taimina, Daina. *Crocheting Adventures with the Hyperbolic Planes.*
   A K Peters, Ltd. Wellesley, MA. 2009.
Tolle, Eckhart. *A New Earth: Awakening to Your Life's Purpose.*
   Plume, A Penguin Publishing Group. 2005.
Walters, Marianne, Betty Carter, Peggy Papp, and Olga Silverstein.
   The Invisible Web: Gender Patterns in Family Relationships. Guil-
   ford Press. NY. 1988.
Wilber, Ken. *Sex, Ecology, Spirituality: The Spirit of Evolution.*
   Shambhala Publications. Boston, MA. 2000.

Websites
www.theiff.org/oexhibits. Website featuring photos and text explaining
   Dr. Taimina's crocheted model of hyperbolic space.
www.mythinglinks.org. Website maintained by Kathleen Jenks, Ph.D.,
   faculty member of Pacifica Graduate Institute. Excellent background on myths and lore regarding fibre connections.
www.suite101.com/article.cfm/jungian_psychology/94231 offers a
   discussion of Jung's concepts of archetypes.

www.arachnology.org. Catalog of topics related to spiders, spider silk.

DVDs

Green, Brian. *The Elegant Universe.* PBS special on *Nova,* 2003. Theoretical physicist Dr. Green explains the complex theory of strings in almost comprehensible ways!

Audiocassettes

Character and Destiny: Authentic Threads in Life. James Hillman and Michael Meade. Pacific Grove, CA: Oral Tradition, 1997. Hillman and Meade discuss our daimon, or calling, through story and poetry.

CHAPTER 2 — FIBRES, OUR SUBSTANCE

Credits

26 Quotation. Thich Nhat Hahn. *Being Peace.* Parallax Press. Berkeley, CA. 2005.

Images

18 Heavenly fleece. Sophie's farm. Minnesota.
22 Bamboo. Wikimedia images. Creative Commons.CC-BY-SA-2.5.
23 *Straw into Gold* by Anne Anderson (1874-1930) http://www.artsy-craftsy.com/anderson_prints.html [Public domain], via Wikimedia Commons.
24 Man with cotton courtesy of Greta Blue, www.gretablue.co.uk. United Kingdom.
25 DNA scarf by Joy Chan, http://joyblogging.typepad.com/joyousknits. Hong Kong.
27 My grandchildren courtesy of their parents. Minnesota.
27 Bird nest courtesy of Laura Erickson, www.lauraerickson.com. Minnesota.
29 Kyrgystan spinner. Photographer: Snell Rullman. Courtesy of Snow Leopard Trust, www.snowleopard.org.
29 Mongolian spinners. Courtesy of Nancy Shands at Nomad Yarns. Altan Chimmmig, photographer. www.nomadyarns.com.

Books

Blood, Charles L., and Martin Link. *The Goat in the Rug.* Parents' Magazine Press. NY. 1986.
Evans, Miriama, Ranui Ngarimu, Norman Heke Photography. *The Art of Maori Weaving: The Eternal Thread.* Huia Publishers. New Zealand. 2005.
Hillman, James. *The Soul's Code: In Search of Character and Calling.* Random House. NY. 1996.
Kingsolver, Barbara. *Small Wonder: Essays.* Perennial Press. NY. 2002.
Schoeser, Mary. *World Textiles: A Concise History.* Thames and Hudson World of Art.London. 2003.

Websites

www.naturalfibres2009.org is the website for the United Nations International Year of Natural Fibres, 2009.
Check www.npr.org/templates/story.php?storyid= for an article entitled *Spider Wranglers Weave One-Of-A-Kind Tapestry.* American Museum of Natural History. September 27, 2009.

Films

A Woman of Substance. 1984 film based on Barbara Taylor Bradford's novel about Emma Harte, who rose from lowly station to head of the textile industry in England.
The Sundowners. 1960 film about Australian sheep ranchers.

The Thornbirds. 1977 film about Australian ranchers, included here because there are scenes of sheep shearing.

CHAPTER 3 — SPINNING POWER AND INNOCENCE

Credits

35 Quotation. Marianne Williamson. *A Woman's Worth.* Random House. 1993.
38 Quotation. Thich Nhat Hahn. *Peace Is Every Step: The Path of Mindfulness in Everyday Life.* Bantam Books. New York. 1992.
38 Quotation. Rollo May. *Power and Innocence: A Search for the Sources of Violence.* Delta Publishing. NY. 1972.

Images

30 *Children of the World* tapestry fabric courtesy of Regal Fabrics, Inc., Massachusetts.
31 Chi Chi bear courtesy of P$YNNER by Chi Chi Amor 2010, www.chichiamor.com. Recycled Guatemalan fabric.
35 Love Blanket, courtesy of The Advocacy Project, www.advocacynet.org.
36 Gandhi. Google Images. Public domain. Source: gandhiserve.org.
36 *The Spinner* by William-Adolphe Bouguereau. commons.wikimedia.org/wiki/Category:1873.
37 *Gandhi Spinning* painting by Sandy Frazier, www.mysticart.com. New York.
37 *Khadi* shirts courtesy of Aniyan Exports, www.aniyanexports.com. Kerala, India.
38 Labyrinth at Te Moata Retreat in Tairua, New Zealand. Photographer Lorna Tomes, Australia.
39 Monkeys and children's items, courtesy of Global Exchange, www.globalexchange.org.

Books

Belenky, Mary Field, Blythe McVicker Clinchy, Nancy Rule Goldberger, Jill Mattuck Tarule. *Women's Ways of Knowing: The Development of Self, Voice, and Mind.* Basic Books. NY. 1986.
Brothers Grimm. *Rumpelstiltskin.* Retold by Paul O. Zelinsky. Puffin Books. New York. 1996.
Steinem, Gloria. *Revolution from Within: A Book of Self-Esteem.* Little, Brown and Company. Boston. 1992.

Websites

www.mayanhands.org is a fair-trade organization working to empower Mayan women in their struggle to overcome poverty.
WARP, an acronym for Weave a Real Peace, is an organization aiming toward networking and empowering textile artists and peace activists across the globe. www.weavearealpeace.org.
For statistics on violence toward women across the globe, check out www.feminist.com.
Another resource for anti-violence action is Friendship Bridge, an organization benefiting Guatemalan women through microcredit and education. www.friendshipbridge.org.
www.fabriclink.com is an index for fibre information, emphasizing sustainable practices.

Films

Gandhi. 1982. Insightful biographical film tracing Gandhi's evolution from young lawyer to leader of nonviolent resistance in India's independence movement.

CHAPTER 4 — THREADS OF IDENTITY

Credits

50 Quotation. John O'Donohue. *To Bless the Space Between Us: A Book of Blessings.* Doubleday. NY. 2008.

52 Quotation. Thich Nhat Hahn. *Calming the Fearful Mind: A Zen Response to Terrorism.* Edited by Rachel Neuman. Parallax Press. CA. 2005.

Images

42 Banjaras, Kishkindha. Courtesy of photographer Ankur Betageri, Bengaluru, India. www.flickr.com.

44 Vikings tennis team. Photograph by coach John Muus. Courtesy of team members Molly Zafft, Cecilia Schnobrich, Audrey Summers, and their parents. Grand Marais, Minnesota.

45 Gulabi Gang of India. Courtesy of Fame Pictures, Inc. www.famepictures.com.

46 Hmong friends. Courtesy of Ying Xiong.

46 Mayan women. Yucatan, Mexico.

47 Amatenango potter courtesy of photographer Thomas Aleto. Ilhulcamina Photo.

48 *Las Abejas huipil.* Chiapas, Mexico.

49 *Mother in Burqa.* Kabul, Afghanistan. Courtesy of photographer Jonathan Wilson. (jbweasle).

51 *Belonging.* Chiapas, Mexico.

52 Orgosolo folk costume of Orgosolo in Sardinia. www.flickr.com/photos/critianocani/2457120918/. Creative Commons, Wikimedia. Sardinia.

53 Drawing by Maryl Skinner.

Books

Allport, Gordon W. *The Nature of Prejudice.* Addison Wesley Longman. NY. 1994.

Briggs, John. *Fractals: The Patterns of Chaos.* Simon and Schuster. NY. 1992.

Gonzales, Ramelle (Romelia). *Threads Breaking the Silence: Stories of the Women of the CPR-Sierra from the Civil War in Guatemala.* Foundations for Education, Inc. Guatemala. 2005.

Jordan, Judith V., Alexandra G. Kaplan, Jean Baker Miller, Irene P. Stiver, and Janet L. Surrey. *Women's Growth in Connection: Writings from the Stone Center.* The Guilford Press. NY. 1991.

McClure, Bud A. *Putting a New Spin on Groups: The Science of Chaos.* Lawrence Erlbaum Associates Inc. U.S. 2005.

Ortiz, Teresa. *Never Again, A World Without Us: Voices of Mayan Women in Chiapas, Mexico.* Epica Task Force. 2001.

See, Lisa. *Snow Flower and the Secret Fan.* Random House. NY. 2006.

Websites

Threads of Yunnan is a project working to improve living conditions for women of Yunnan Province, China. The colorful fibre projects are for sale at www.danyun.com.

Films

Water is the third in a series done by Deepa Mehta. It is a deeply moving story about widows in traditional Indian society. All three films —*Fire, Earth,* and *Water*—caused protest in India.

CHAPTER 5 — BRAIDING INTIMATE CORDS

Credits

64 Quotation. Thich Nhat Hanh. *Touching Peace: Practicing the Art of Mindful Living. Revised edition. Parallax Press. CA. 2009.*

Images

56 Braided scarves designed and photographed by Maryl Skinner.

58 Children's friendship bracelets courtesy of Larisa Yagolnitser, www.KidsKnitwork.com. California.

60 Peruvian friendship bracelets courtesy of photographer Matt Huusko, www.MonsterTrendz.com. New Hampshire.

62 Korfbol courtesy of Professor Marcos Diaz, www.uruguayeduca.edu.uy. Uruguay. From Wikimedia commons.

63 Guatemalan braids. Courtesy of Education and More, www.educationandmore.com. Karen Pickett, photographer.

64 *Female After the Bath* by Edgar Degas. Awesome Art, www.awesome-art.biz/awesome.

65 *The Tub* by Edgar Degas. Google Images. Licensed by Creative Commons. Creativecommons.org/licenses.

66 Rapunzel scarves by Barbara Mowery, www.bbmowery.blogspot.com.

Books

Andes, Karen. *A Woman's Book of Power: Using Dance to Cultivate Energy and Health in Mind, Body, and Spirit.* The Berkley Publishing Group. NY. 1998.

Damasio, Antonio. *The Feeling of What Happens: Body and Emotion in the Making of Consciousness.* A Harvest Book: Harcourt, Inc. San Diego. 2000.

Montagu, Ashley. *Touching: The Human Significance of the Skin.* 3rd edition. Harper & Row. NY. 1971.

Pert, Candace, Ph.D. *Molecules of Emotion: The Science Behind Mind-Body Medicine.* Touchstone. 1999.

Websites

www.anapsid.org/cnd/gender/tendfend.html is Melissa Kaplan's site regarding chronic neuroimmune diseases. It includes Gale Berkowitz's article regarding the UCLA study on women's friendships and the stress response.

Films

The following films address the importance of friendships, especially among women.
Beaches
The Color Purple
Fried Green Tomatoes
How to Make an American Quilt
Steel Magnolias
The Visitor
The Women of Brewster Place

CHAPTER 6 — COLORS OF CREATIVITY

Credits

73 Quotation. Thich Nhat Hahn. *Being Peace.* Parallax Press. Berkeley, CA. 2005.

73 Quotation. Richard Bergland. *Fabric of Mind.* Penguin. NY. 1989.

Images

68 *Green Hills* needle felting by Debra Poth, www.deebs.etsy.com. Washington.

70 Sweaters by Erika Mock at www.erikamock.com. Wisconsin.

71 Sweaters by Erika Mock, website above.

72 Iris Bauermeister and Karen Lohn. Works by Iris at www.etsy.com/shop/WearableWhimsy. Mahtomedi, Minnesota.

74 Weaving by Mary Fechner. Adrian, Michigan.

75 Linda Bauer, www.ravensbeakdesign.com. Grand Marais, Minnesota.

76 Luna shawl with poppies by Inger Maaike, www. ingermaaike@etsy. http:/commons.wikimedia.org/wiki/File:NunoFelt_by_ingermaaike2.jpg. Norway.

77 Mittens with poppies by Inger Maaike, website above.

78 Quilted journal by Marci Glenn at Simply Artistic Pleasures, www.marciglenn.wordpress.com. Oregon.

79 *Stone Soup Woman* by Julie Muscha, Iowa. Wrapped by K. Lohn.

80 *Jeanne* fabric sculpture by Lisa Lichtenfels, www.lisalichtenfels.net. Massachusetts.

81 Fabric garden sculpture by Kathryn Fudge, www.paverpolvancouverisland.blogspot.com. Vancouver.

81 *African Lady* fabric sculpture by Merilyn Thomas, www.sculpturebymerilyn.com.au. Australia.

83 *Chakra Healing Blanket* by Steve Attwood-Wright at De Mont & Wright Studio, Lower View, Sarn, Powys, SY16 4HH, UK 01686 670793. £200 per blanket + postage. U.K.

Websites

View a sampling of Erika Mock's work and visit her workshop schedule at www.erikamock.com.

Fibre artist Brenna Busse's creative work can be viewed at www.BrennaBusse.com. Brenna is a colleague of Erika Mock.

Iris Bauermeister's vibrant creations can be found at www.etsy.com/shop/WearableWhimsy.

Learn about the extensive brain research done by Dr. Roger Sperry at www.rogersperry.org.

Books

Cameron, Julia. *The Artist's Way: A Spiritual Path to Higher Creativity.* Tarcher/Putnam. NY. 1992.

Edwards, Betty. *Drawing on the Right Side of the Brain: A Course in Enhancing Creativity and Artistic Confidence.* Tarcher. Los Angeles. 1979.

Fox, Matthew. *Creativity: Where the Divine and the Human Meet.* Tarcher/Putnam. NY. 2002.

Gawain, Shakti. *Creative Visualization Meditations.* New World Library. 2002.

Myss, Caroline. *Anatomy of the Spirit: Seven Stages of Power and Healing.* Crown Publishers. NY. 1996.

Ornstein, Robert. *The Right Mind: Making Sense of the Hemispheres.* Harcourt Brace. NY. 1997.

Sark. *Succulent Wild Woman: Dancing with Your Wonder-full Self.* Simon Schuster. NY. 1997.

Sark. *Make Your Creative Dream Real: A Plan for Procrastinators, Perfectionists, Busy People, and People Who Would Rather Sleep All Day.* Simon and Schuster. NY. 2004.

Taylor, Jill Bolte, Ph.D. *My Stroke of Insight: A Brain Scientist's Personal Journey.* Viking Press. NY. 2008.

CHAPTER 7 — WEAVING DIVERSITY

Credits

86 *Weave* hymn. Copyright 1979. Rosemary Crow, used with permission. North Carolina.

88 Quotation. Howard Bloom. *Global Brain: The Evolution of Mass Mind from the Big Bang to the 21st Century.* John Wiley & Sons. 2000.

88 Quotation. Margaret Fuller. *Woman in the Nineteenth Century.* Harvard University Library. 1845.

97 Quotation and "Weaver's Song" used with permission. Bennett, Noël and Tiana Bighorse. *Navajo Weaving Way: The Path from Fleece to Rug.* Interweave Press. Loveland, CO. 1997.

98 Quotation. Maya Angelou. *Maya Angelou: Diversity Makes for a Rich Tapestry.* Donna Brown Agins. Enslow Publishers. N.J. 2006.

Images

84 *Fabric of a Nation* watercolor by Larisa Sembaliuk Cheladyn from the Celebrating Women collection commissioned by the National Council of Women of Canada. www.artbylarisa.com; www.ncwc.ca.

86 Fibre pieces, pages 86-89, courtesy of Uwe Stuecher, Ph.D., University of Minnesota, Duluth, Minnesota.

87 Masumi, crest courtesy of Masumi Goto Stuecher, Duluth, Minnesota.

90 Tomas with needlepoint courtesy of Tomas Hardy. St. Paul, Minnesota.

91 *Sophia's Mantle* courtesy of Terry Helwig, www.thethreadproject.com. Florida.

93 *Quilt Woman* painting by Tarah Rowse, francisbarnhart.com/blog/2005/03/06/tarah_paintings/. Belize.

94 Photo of dancer by Michael Cairns, Wet Orange Studios. Property of Orlando Ballet. Dancer: Chiaki Yasukawa. Used with permission. Florida.

95 Yoga Tree Pose courtesy of Esther Ekhart, www.yogatic.com, and photographer Ruud Voerman, www.ruudvoerman.nl. Netherlands.

96 *Kente* weavers courtesy of Aurora Fox, http://foxyartstudio.blogspot.com. Oregon and Alaska.

96 Weaving courtesy of Mary MacDonald. www.creative.com. Grand Marais, Minnesota.

96 Assamese weaver. Photographer Deepraj. 2006 Wikimedia Creative Commons 3.0. Tespur, India.

99 Bob's flies courtesy of Bob Lohn. Minnesota.

Websites

Terry Helwig's website, including an amazing photo album of the global weaving project, is www.threadproject.com.

Learn more about Qigong, an ancient Eastern practice, taught by Master Chunyi Lin. The exercise is adapted from his teachings. www.springforestqigong.com.

www.marshall.edu/akanart/cloth_kente.html. This gives a synopsis of the history, techniques, and symbolism of the weaving of *kente* cloth.

www.wool.com. A glimpse at the many aspects of wool production.

Books

Baldwin, John D., and Janice I. Baldwin. *Behavior Principles in Everyday Life.* Fourth edition. Prentice Hall. NJ. 2001.

Beck, Don Edward, and Christopher C. Cowan. *Spiral Dynamics: Mastering Values, Leadership, and Change.* Blackwell Publishing. NJ. 2005.

Chocolate, Debbi. *Kente Colors.* Walker Books for Young Readers. 1997. Illustrated by John Ward.

Fox, Matthew, and Rupert Sheldrake. *Natural Grace: Dialogues on Creation, Darkness, and the Soul in Spirituality and Science.* Doubleday. NY. 1996.

McQuiston, Don and Debra, with text by Lynne Bush and photography by Tom Till. *The Woven Spirit of the Southwest.* Chronicle Books. San Francisco. 1995.

Pomar, Maria Teresa, and Juan Rafael Coronel Rivera. *Maya Textile Art: Collections of the Centro de Textiles del MUNDO MAYA.* Artesf Graficas Polermo workshops under the supervision of Turner Pulicaciones, S.I. 2006.

CHAPTER 8 — YARNS OF GENERATIVITY

Credits

102 Quotation. Poem from *The Heart of God: Prayers of Rabindranath Tagore,* selected and edited by Herbert F. Vetter. 1997. Reprinted with express permission of Tuttle Publishing.

108 Quotation. Thich Nhat Hahn. *Present Moment, Wonderful Moment: Mindfulness Verses for Daily Living.* Parallax Press. CA. 1990.

Images

100 Bujumbura women sewing, © photographer Jan Oberg. Courtesy Jan Oberg and the Transnational Foundation for Peace and Future Research, www.obergphotograpics.com. Sweden.

102 Dancing brooches courtesy of Sandra Haff and the artists at I Love a Parade: Art Created by Your Homeless Neighbors, www.iloveaparade.org. Minneapolis, Minnesota.

104 Masks courtesy of Sandra Haff. See info above.

104 *Drugs* (split doll) by Sandy. Photograph © 2008 Doug Knutson. dougknutson.com; www.NobelPeacePortraits.com. *The Dolls: Women who have experienced homelessness tell their stories through art.* By the artists of I Love a Parade. 2008.

105 *Confusion* (lightning doll) by Michell. See info above.

106 Sweaters for Chiapas courtesy of Mary Igoe and others. Grand Marais, Minnesota.

108 Decorative boxes by Maryl Skinner.

109 Freeset page courtesy of John Sinclair at www.freesetglobal.com. England and Wales.

111 Sewing machine courtesy of Katie Zdechlik. White Bear Lake, Minnesota.

Websites

Visit Sandra Haff's organizational site, www.iloveaparade.org. You will view many of the unique creations, hear artists' stories, and learn about the organization.

www.heifer.org is the website of my favorite global charity organization. The philosophy of ongoing benefits derived from animals encourages recipients' competence and capacity for self-sufficiency. Sheep, goats, llamas, silk worms, baskets of yarn are provided to families.

For information on an organized effort to end world hunger, go to www.bread.org.

www.projectlinus.org creates and places handmade blankets and quilts in hospitals for children.

Assisting women in Afghanistan in a variety of ways, including knitting needles for the blind, is the mission at www.alittlehelp.org.

Serving war-torn Afghanistan, www.afghansforafghans.org directs the making and shipping of handmade items for that country.

The handwork of women working to provide for their families is sold at www.worldofgood.com.

www.ragdolls2love.org is a Mary Page Jones' website for her non-profit organization sending hand-stitched dolls to children in war-torn countries.

Books

Erikson, Erik H., Joan M. Erikson, and Helen Q. Kivnick. *Vital Involvement in Old Age.* W.W. Norton and Co. NY. 1986.

Gardiner, Harry S., and Corinne Kosmitzki. *Lives Across Cultures: Cross-Cultural Human Development.* Allyn and Bacon. Fourth edition. 2007.

Hen Co-op, The. *Growing Old Disgracefully: New Ideas for Getting the Most Out of Life.* The Crossing Press. Freedom, CA. 1994.

CHAPTER 9 — STITCHING THROUGH CRISES

Credits

115 Quotation. William Bridges. *Transitions: Making Sense of Life's Changes.* Revised 25th Anniversary edition. Da Capo Press. MA. 2004.

120 Quotation. Mary I. Farr. *If I Could Mend Your Heart...!* N.K. Books. Book Peddlers. Minnetonka, MN. 2001.

121 Quotation. Rachel Naomi Remen. *My Grandfather's Blessings.* Riverhead Books. NY. 2000.

122 Quotation. Thich Nhat Hanh. *Being Peace.* Parallax Press. Berkeley, CA. 2005.

Images

112 Arm quilt by Dana Warner Fisher, *The Quilted Librarian,* http://danawarnerfisher.blogspot.com. North Carolina.

114 Breast cancer quilt by Suzanne Marshall, www.suzannequilts.com. Missouri.

119 Words of comfort by Joetta Maue, www.joettamaue.com; www.littleyellowbirds.blogspot.com. New York.

120 Arm quilt with Dan courtesy of Dana Fisher. See above.

121 *Twin Towers* beadwork by Robin Atkins, www.robinatkins.com and beadlust.blogspot.com. Washington.

122 Serenity Prayer cut paper design by Cathy Fauss, www.myserenityway.com. New York.

Books

Csikszentmihalyi, Mihaly. *FLOW: The Psychology of Optimal Experience.* Harper Perennial. NY. 1997.

Kaplan, Connie. *The Invisible Garment: 30 Spiritual Principles that Weave the Fabric of Life.* Jodere Publishing Group. CA. 2004.

Kubler-Ross, Elisabeth, *On Death and Dying.* Touchstone. NY. 1969.

Love, Susan. *Dr. Susan Love's Breast Book.* 3rd edition. Harper Collins. NY. 2000.

James, John W. and Russell Friedman. T*he Grief Recovery Handbook: The Action Program for Moving Beyond Death, Divorce, and Other Losses.* Harper Collins. NY. 1998.

Moore, Mary Carroll. *How to Master Change in Your Life: Sixty-seven Ways to Handle Life's Toughest Moments.* Eckankar. MN. 1997.

Schafer, Walt. *Stress Management for Wellness.* 4th edition. Wadsworth. CA. 1998.

Wilber, Ken, and Treya Killam Wilber. *Grace and Grit: Spirituality and Healing in the Life and Death of Treya Killam Wilber.* Shambhala Publications. Boston, MA. 1989.

Websites

Journeys: A Newsletter to Help in Bereavement. The Hospice Foundation of America. www.hospicefoundation.org. Helpful reading, but, more importantly, a connection to the tremendous services available through the Hospice Foundation.

www.shawlministy.com not only tells the history of the prayer shawl ministry, but offers links to specific ones and directions for setting up a ministry.

CHAPTER 10 — RIPPING OUT, RESILIENCE

Credits

132 Quotation. Mary Kay Blakely. *Quilting New Networks* in *Ms. Magazine.* March/April, 1992.

133 Quotation. Rachel Naomi Remen. *My Grandfather's Blessings.* Riverhead Books. NY. 2000.

Images

126 Crazy quilt courtesy of Maryl Skinner.

128 Journal Quilt panels by Melissa Devin. See website below.

129 Journal Quilt by Melissa Devin, atypicalquilter@thedevins.com and http://solje.thedevins.com/blog. Washington.

130 Slave quilt, 1846. Gwen Ellis, owner. Purchase information: Julia Kelly-Hodenius, Piqué, www.piquetrouver.com. Georgia.

130 Collage by Katrina Parker, 2004. Photo courtesy of Kerry Davis. www.louisianafolklife.org/quilts/features/parker_family_quilt_heritage. Louisiana.

131 *History with No Memory* by Karen S. Musgrave, http://connectionsbykaren.blogspot.com. Illinois.

132 *Children of Sichuan Province* by Hazel Chiu, www.hazelchiu.com. Hong Kong.

133 Humility blocks, quilt squares with error by Nicole Shyne Reed, www.sisterschoicequilts.typepad.com. California.

134 *Living Positively by Design* courtesy of Jack Mackenroth, spokesperson for Living Positively by Design and the Names AIDS Quilt Project, http://blog.jackmackenroth.com. New York.

135 *Leaving Us* quilt by Cheryl Lynch, author of !Quilt Fiesta! Used by permission. www.CherylLynchQuilts.com. Pennsylvania.

136 *Torn Fabric Series* by Laura Kamian McDermott, www.laurakamian.com. California.

137 Little Dresses for Africa photo courtesy of Ashley Photography and Rachel O'Neill, www.littledressesforafrica. Michigan.

137 *Rolled* by students of Path with Art in collaboration with Recovery Café, courtesy of teaching artist, Lucas Deon Spivey, www.pathwithart.org. Washington.

138 Wrapped frame courtesy of Doug Hemer. Stillwater, Minnesota.

Books

Bridges, William. *Transitions: Making Sense of Life's Changes.* Revised 25th Anniversary edition. Da Capo Press. MA. 2004.

Didion, Joan. *A Year of Magical Thinking.* Knopf. 2005.

Hughes, Mary Willette. *Quilt Pieces.* North Star Press of St. Cloud. 2001.

Polacco, Patricia. *The Keeping Quilt.* Aladdin Paperbacks. 2001.

Rogers, Carl. *On Becoming a Person.* Houghton Mifflin. 1961.

Websites

www.amaniafrica.org. "Where peace is sewn through the eye of a needle." Sewing and reconciliation project for marginalized women in Africa.

www.aidsquilt.com explains the motivation and achievement of the AIDS quilt project.

www.apahelpcenter.org is a resource established by the American Psychological Association offering multilingual assistance in locating help as well as giving tips for dealing with stress and trauma.

Visit www.quiltsofgeesbend.com for a complete history, gallery, and links to additional sites regarding these fantastic Gee's Bend quilts.

http://e-aceh-nias.org is a site hosted by the UN Development Fund for Women whose goal is "Equality and Freedom from Poverty and Violence." There is a lengthy report on steps taken in Banda Aceh following the 2006 tsunami.

Celebrating the 100 year anniversary of International Women's Day in 2011, quilts were created and are now on display at the United nations in Switzerland. Visit www.quiltchallenge.org to learn more.

Films

The Wizard of Oz. Watch the original 1939 version or an updated one to see the emergence of resilience in all of the characters.

CHAPTER 11 — TAPESTRIES OF INTEGRATION

Credits

142 *Weave* hymn. Copyright 1979. Rosemary Crow, used with permission. North Carolina.

146 Quotation. Uma Silbey. *Enlightenment on the Run: Everyday Life as a Spiritual Path.* Airo Press. 1993. CA.

148 Quotation. Thich Nhat Hahn. *Present Moment, Wonderful Moment: Mindfulness Verses for Daily Living.* Parallax Press. CA. 1990.

Images

140 Border from tapestry by Ulrika Leander. See 146 below, *Lovers.*

140 *People in Chains* Chilean *arpillera* by Gala Torres, courtesy of Margaret Snook at www.cachandochile.com. Santiago de Chile.

143 *Looking Out the Window, arpillera* by Violeta Morales, courtesy of Margaret Snook, www.cachandochile.com. Santiago de Chile.

143 *Transformation Spirits* by Gloria Inuguq Putumiraqtuq. Baker Lake, Nunavut, Canada. Courtesy of Elaine Blechman, www.articartistry.com. New York.

144 *Minstrel of Souls* painting by Freydoon Rassouli. Used with permission. www.Rassouli.com. California.

145 United States Geological Survey (USGS) tapestry courtesy of USGS, http://tapestry.usgs.gov/physiogr/physio.html.

146 *The Flaw in the Persian Carpet* used by permission of photographer Andrew Marjoribanks, www.dpchallenge.com. South Africa.

146 *Lovers* tapestry by Swedish artist Ulrika Leander, www.ctw-tapestry.com. Photographer Tom Miller. Maryland.

148 Ulrika Leander in yarns photographed by Kirsten Beckerman. Maryland.

149 Bac Ha Market courtesy of Luc Suerin, www.flickr.com. Babylas 123 photostream. France.

149 Textiles from Bhutan courtesy of Judie Johnson. Grand Marais, Minnesota.

151 Dolls courtesy of women of First Congregational Church, Grand Marais, Minnesota.

Books

Gianturco Paolah, and Toby Tuttle. *In Her Hands: Craftswomen Changing the World.* Penguin Press. 2000.

Gipson, Morrell. *The Surprise Doll.* Wonder Books. NY. 1949.

Cha, Dia. *Dia's Story Cloth: the Hmong People's Journey of Freedom.* Lee and Low Books, NY. 1996.

Websites

The stories portrayed in the *arpilleras* of Chile are at www.cachandochile.com. Following the military coup of September 11, 1973, martial law resulted in mistreatment and disappearances. Women expressed their angst and activism through their stitched *arpilleras.*

View gorgeous fibre collages created by Asian women at www.aawaa.org.

"Jan's gallery" is Sivertson Gallery, Grand Marais, Minnesota. It features art of the north at www.sivertson.com.

The Kilim/eCommerce School of Ortahisar/Barbara Sher website at www.kilimwomen.com includes history, pictorials, and an opportunity to contribute to or purchase these Turkish rugs.

Woven, Not Carved: The Pangnirtung Tapestries are Northern Art with Global Appeal, by L.D. Cross in *ARCTIC,* Volume 56, NO.3, September, 2003, p. 310-316. This article about the relatively new Inuit art form of weaving can also be found by typing "pangnirtung tapestry" into your browser.

Women Who Dare, a film by Binnur Karaevli, is previewed at www.eastwestdocumentary.com, with historical background about women in Turkey as well as about three women who challenge old views and restrictions. One of the women is an accomplished textile artist and psychologist.

Magazines

Cloth, Paper, Scissors: Cloth, Mixed Media, Artistic Discovery contains innovative ideas and articles exciting to fibre artists of all sorts.

"A Stitch in Time" by Julie Caniglia in *The Rake,* November, 2005, pages 44ff. This article describes Jessica Rankin's unusual tapestries linking the cosmic and the mundane.

Films

Threads of Hope is a documentary about the lives of the people of Chile after the military coup; it features the women who created *arpilleras* to depict the plight of the missing and lost. Narrated by Donald Sutherland. 1996.

CHAPTER 12 — CELEBRATING THE FABRIC OF LIFE

Credits

154 Quotation. Karen Andes. *A Woman's Book of Power: Using Dance to Cultivate Energy and Health in Mind, Body, and Spirit.* The Berkley Publishing Group. NY. 1998.

161 Quotation. Thich Nhat Hahn. *Touching Peace: Practicing the Art of Mindful Living.* Parallax Press. 1993.

Images

152 Border from painted fabric by Ann Johnston, www.annjohnston.net. Washington.

152 Color Wheel Dancers courtesy of photographer Carl F. Sermon Photography, www.CarlSermonPhotography; Zenfolio.com; www.ReelSoundandLight.com; and Patricia Aishah Rusich, www.meetup.com/SF-Bay-Area-Dance-4-Positivity-Living-Breathing-Colorwheel. California.

154 Mayan altar courtesy of Robert Sitler, http://www.stetson.edu/~rsitler/ or http://robertsitler.com. Florida.

155 Yaya dancing photo courtesy of Kerri Biller, www.blackbearmoon.com. New Hampshire.

158 Prayer flags courtesy of photographer Bob Pranis, bpranis.smugmug.com; bpranis@northlc.com. Grand Marais, Minnesota.

159 *War and Peace* by Melanie Johnston, http://qcartquilts.blogspot.com/2010/10/found-objects.html. Connecticut.

160 *Viva La Gong Tree* by Denise Litchfield, www.grrlandog.com. Sydney, Australia.

162 Batiks courtesy of Korey Thompson and Bonnie Gay Hedstrom. Grand Marais, Minnesota.

162 Batiks drying at Cape Ha, Yucatan, Mexico.

163 Batik courtesy of Judy Siegle, Grand Marais, Minnesota.

164 Coral Reef Project used with permission of the Institute For Figuring, www.theiff.org. California.

165 Photo of Dr. Daina Taimina courtesy of Leina Spigana. Iceland.

166 *Ribbon Dance* courtesy of photographer Dan Heller, www.danheller.com. California.

167 "Daandia Raas, Folk Dance Of Gujarat" courtesy of Exotic India, www.exoticindiaart.com. India.

167 *Reach for the Stars* batik by Suzanne Drown, www.etsy.com/listing/22153184/reach-for-the-stars-batik-print. Maine.

Books

Arthur, Linda B., editor. *Undressing Religion: Commitment and Conversion from a Cross-Cultural Perspective.* Berg Publishers. 2000.

Fox, Matthew, and Rupert Sheldrake. *Natural Grace: Dialogues on Creation, Darkness, and the Soul in Spirituality and Science.* Image Books. Doubleday. NY. 1999.

Kertzer, David. *Ritual, Politics, and Power.* Yale University. 1988.

Seligman, Martin E.P. *Authentic Happiness: Using the New Positive Psychology to Realize Your Potential for Lasting Fulfillment.* Simon and Schuster. NY. 2002.

Websites

At www.boldoverbatiks.com, you will learn about a Malaysian project to provide a living wage for batik artists.

Films

Elizabeth I, the 2005 television movie starring Helen Mirren, offers visual evidence of the role of opulent clothing in the British monarchy.

Memoirs of a Geisha offers rich viewing of the elaborate silk work of the *geishas.*

AFTERTHREAD

Images

168 Border from silk fabric, hand dyed by Linda Monaghan Sands. Florida.

168 *Art Deco* fabric sculpture by Merilyn Thomas, www.sculpturebymerilyn.com.au. Australia.

169 Scrunch ball by Catherine Zdechlik.

PRODUCTION BABY

I eagerly await the arrival of my next grandchild, Andy and Erika's daughter, who is due by press time. —K.L.

ENVIRONMENTAL BENEFITS STATEMENT

Karen Lohn saved the following resources by printing the pages of this book on chlorine free paper made with 10% post-consumer waste.

TREES	WATER	SOLID WASTE	GREENHOUSE GASES
4	1,913	116	397
FULLY GROWN	GALLONS	POUNDS	POUNDS

Calculations based on research by Environmental Defense and the Paper Task Force. Manufactured at Friesens Corporation